## What People of A

## About Frank Raj's Poems

## *A Spiritual Traveler*

Frank's poems are sincere and straightforward, and a line from one captures the essence for me: *I am weary of a world divided as Hindus, Muslims, Christians, Jews.* That Frank considers the adherents of *all* religions to be equally in search of Truth (*satyam, nityam,* and *anantham,* in Upanishadic texts) is amply evident. I admire his *bhakti* and *shraddha* and say this with the highest respect.

—**Prema Raghunath,** Chennai, India, author of *The Cousins*

Frank Raj's poetry reflects the dignity and grace of his fascinating spiritual journey. Simple and direct, the verses resound with sheer power as they question age-old ideas and beliefs with extraordinary vision and insight.

—**Ikram Shikooh,** a Dubai-based media consultant

Frank takes us on a journey as he peels the spiritual away from the ritual, forcing the reader to focus on the essence of faith. His style of poetry is gentle, and without realizing it, his journey becomes ours. *A Spiritual Traveler* is a must-read for anyone trying to get beyond the superficial practice of faith that focuses on tribalism and division.

—**Satjit Singh,** Visiting Lecturer at Bayes Business School, London

Frank beautifully crafts a spiritual journey in poetry so inspirational he gets you to think and reconsider your own. You read a poem, then reread it, as every verse is independently fascinating, even as it links to another verse. His book engages

you in a personal, soul-binding experience reliving one's spiritual journey and seeing it unfold.
—**George Metry,** Program Manager, Washington, DC

Frank Raj's poetry is a beautiful mix of the spiritual, the personal, and the political. I found him when he penned an entire poem as an amazing review of my book. Read his poetry to join his fascinating journey of the self and the inner self.
—**Debasish Roy Chowdhury,** journalist and co-author of *To Kill a Democracy: India's Passage to Despotism*

Frank urges us to seek the Truth; no holds barred. He calls a spade a spade and has no qualms about doing so. His words are a clarion call to our interpretation of religion and spirituality. The strength and beauty of his poems lie in the way they take us to the depths of our consciousness, our inner self. Stark, yet they gently and firmly compel us to take stock of the world around us... peel away the layers... and introspect to find the hidden Truth.
—**Bushra Alvi Razzack,** Delhi, India, writer, poet, and editor of *Dilliwali: Celebrating the Woman of Delhi through Poetry*

Frank's poems, while spiritual, appeal because they stress the need for peace and brotherhood, so fractured in recent times because of the weaponization of organized religion. I appreciate his understanding of Christ as The Way vis a vis Christianity, the religion. May his poems be the harbinger of peace between people.
—**Melanie P. Kumar**, independent writer based in Bangalore, India

Frank is at his best when clearing the mists around living life in keeping with the tenets of faith; he writes with a firm hand and a clear eye on relevant issues and troubling ambiguities. Unafraid of rocking the boat occasionally, he is a candid voice to hear in the future.

—**Bobby Kishore Gambeer,** an avid storyteller who loves fascinating tales when he's not selling dates (the edible ones) to customers from his Los Angeles base

# God Calling in Poetry

## A Devotional for 365 Days
## for Doubting, Troubled Hearts

# God Calling in Poetry

## A Devotional for 365 Days
## for Doubting, Troubled Hearts

Frank Raj

CIRCLE
BOOKS

Winchester, UK
Washington, USA

First published by Circle Books, 2024
Circle Books is an imprint of Collective Ink Ltd.,
Unit 11, Shepperton House, 89 Shepperton Road, London, N1 3DF
office@collectiveinkbooks.com
www.collectiveinkbooks.com
www.circle-books.com

For distributor details and how to order please visit the 'Ordering' section on our website.



ISBN: 978 1 80341 390 7
978 1 80341 391 4 (ebook)
Library of Congress Control Number: 2023941724



A CIP catalogue record for this book is available from the British Library.

Design: Lapiz Digital Services

UK: Printed and bound by CPI Group (UK) Ltd, Croydon, CR0 4YY
US: Printed and bound by Thomson Shore, 7300 West Joy Road, Dexter, MI 48130

# Contents

*For God speaketh once, yea twice, yet man perceiveth it not.*
*—Job 33:14*

*But seek first his kingdom and his righteousness, and all these things will be given to you as well. Therefore, do not worry about tomorrow, for tomorrow will worry about itself. Each day has enough trouble of its own.*
*—Matthew 6:33–34*

*And without faith it is impossible to please him, for whoever would draw near to God must believe that he exists and that he rewards those who seek him.*
*—Hebrews 11:6*

To my grandchildren, Rivkah, Tirzah, and David, praying they will always stop and listen to God's still, small voice amidst all the distractions and noise.

# Author's Note

I am delighted *God Calling in Poetry* found its way to you. If you find it helpful, would you encourage one more person to read it?

Another follower or friend of the Christ, perhaps even a skeptic.

# Foreword

***Jeremiah 33:3***
*Call unto me, and I will answer thee, and show thee great and mighty things, which thou knowest not.*

*The Scriptures offer no other basis for conversion than the personal magnetism of the Master.*
*— Brennan Manning*

Who doesn't long to converse with the Lord and commune with Him?

Sometimes, my cry has been, Lord, when your Word says you do not show favoritism (Romans 2:11), how come I learn about people connecting with you and feel left out?

And, of course, I know He doesn't ignore any of His children. He certainly hasn't neglected me—in some incredible ways, the Lord revealed Himself at crucial times when I needed Him most. God does not discriminate—He makes us know we are unique, and His interaction is not a one-size-fits-all. He loves everyone equally. James emphasizes that favoritism is not simply disrespectful of people; it is a sin against God (James. 2:9). It is a sin because it is contrary to His character and command.

The stunning fact is there is nothing we can ever do to make God love us more, and there is nothing we can ever do that will make God love us less.

Mother Teresa reportedly observed, "I am a little pencil in the hand of a writing God who is sending a love letter to the world." I figured our Creator, *The Great Poet*, calls us to imitate Him; hence this Bible-inspired book of humble poetry.

Regardless of your spiritual persuasion, *God Calling in Poetry* is a simple book to read and gain powerful biblical insights in small bites every day, regardless of age, culture, or situation.

Today our convictions face daily threats from loud voices in society. Where can we find the Truth? Only from the One who audaciously claimed He is the Way, the Truth, and the Life.

*God Calling* was a bestselling devotional by two British women, one of whom claimed the Lord communicated with her directly. The "Two Listeners," as they are known, published their little devotional anonymously nearly a century ago, reaching millions of readers.

I make no such claim in my book *God Calling in Poetry*. I am a 73-year-old prodigal who, after reluctantly returning to the heavenly Father's home, sneaked out repeatedly before finally deciding I had done enough traveling—what Blaise Pascal called "licking the earth." Pascal also said, "Truth is so obscure in these times, and falsehood so established, that, unless we love the truth, we cannot know it."

Being in the media business for most of my life, I endured the ravages of prosperity and failure on *all* of life's fronts with a modicum of success.

Though I never doubted, always believed, I was a glutton for the good life. Sensual, Self-assured and Success-seeking would have aptly described me. *Many things captured my heart, but only after finally comprehending the wildly extravagant love of God late in life did I find the key to overcoming sin.* Once the penny dropped, I understood why the French greet each other at Easter with "L'amour de Dieu est folie" (The love of God is madness); because only from the love of God arises a longing to be free from sin to cling to the Truth like never before.

So, does the living Christ communicate with us today?

If He didn't, we couldn't *know* Him.

If God doesn't speak to us, how can we have a relationship? How can we understand His incredible Love?

Love not communicated cannot be understood.

My earthly father rarely showed me his love; as a result, I barely knew him.

When many stopped following Jesus, He pointedly asked His disciples, "Do you also want to go away?" If you can say with the Apostle Peter, "Lord, to whom shall we go? You have the words of eternal life," then the conversation begins.

God strategically chose a singular scripture verse to first connect with me:

> ***2 Timothy 1:7***
> *For God hath not given us the spirit of fear; but of power, and of love, and of a sound mind.*

At a time when I had no power or love, robbed as I was of a sound mind.

I can never forget how that life-giving verse got my attention. Slowly I have understood and experienced its powerful impact over the years.

May the Lord uniquely speak to you, too, one day at a time!

*Frank Raj*
*Elkridge*
*Maryland*
*February 14, 2023*

# Acknowledgements

I could not have written *God Calling in Poetry* without help from *The Great Poet.* To the source of all inspiration this is my grateful poem prayer.

Opening Latin words for Simeon's ancient prayer: **Luke 2:29–32**
*Nunc Dimittis servum tuum Domine secundum verbum tuum in pace quia viderunt oculi mei salutare tuum quod parasti ante faciem omnium populorum lumen ad revelationem gentium et gloriam plebis tuae Israhel.*

"Sovereign Lord, as you have promised, you may now dismiss your servant in peace. For my eyes have seen your salvation, which you have prepared in the sight of all nations: a light for revelation to the Gentiles, and the glory of your people Israel."

**Nunc Dimittis**

ANOTHER effort to employ my writing talent from you
More diligently than I've done so far, it is long overdue
Prioritizing affluence and mere comforts a lifetime flew
I just kept chasing goals you didn't equip me to pursue

BLAMING others, I could justify why my talent got buried
But I succumbed to my senses, procrastinated, and worried
Life receded, little to show, my accomplishments ordinary
Three score years and ten I've crossed, too long did I tarry

LORD I am grateful you increased my yield of labor
My body could use healing, and my mind your favor
I start and stop, help me persist in all my endeavors
Ride discipline hard like a drilled war horse to savor

YOU restored the years eaten by the locust I testify
If I can't employ my talents, your gifts from on high
How can I lift you up to do what you said — multiply?
To many you give this privilege, favor me Adonai!

LONG buried talent I've dug up, help me now to apply
To him who has, you promised more, you won't deny
Not for riches or fame but to finish all I conceptualized
My shield, my exceeding great reward, you are my supply

MINE eyes have seen thy salvation and I'm ready to depart
Whenever your time frame for my life requires me to start
But until your summons maximize fresh output from my heart
Help me overcome weaknesses, keep me alert; set me apart

NOTHING exceeds your priceless gift of salvation I received
I seek no higher Calling; only to make you known, believed
To staunchly tell the world what you have done to redeem
Go home knowing you see me faithful, and you are pleased

# January

## January 1

## How I Work

**Hebrews 10:10**
*By the which will we are sanctified through the offering of the body of Jesus Christ once for all.*

Know in My work of sanctifying you; there are two sides
Two contrasting, not contradicting parts, each sits beside
Your responsibility to trust; mine to do the work, provide
For deliverance from sin to perfection, in Me, you abide

Conquering besetting sin, removing routine vices in place
You pursue freedom, and you try to get rid of the menace
Evil haunts you, and you cannot escape from its embrace
I died; you are unchained, not enslaved; Live in My grace

Heed My command in Romans 6:11; you are "dead unto sin"
I will make this a reality; if you trust Me, new life will begin
Sanctification is a spontaneous step and process for My kin
You believe and trust; My responsibility is your redemption

In My Word, I declare I Am the Potter; you are the clay
Mud submits to the Potter's craft; it is work, not play
I knead, fashion, and mold to shape you and cut away
Treasure pain: when gold gets refined, it doesn't decay

You cannot gauge it, but My work is perfect at every stage
There will be times when the battle for your soul will wage
If you set your mind on sin and death, your flesh will rage
Yield yourself wholly to Me; continue trusting in old age

A child obtains parental care, complete and unconditional
But love must soon discipline, as childhood is transitional
My sons and daughters need schooling too, for a life eternal
Till you are home, I too must train; for your flesh is carnal

The woodcutter fells a tree, his axe as a tool to perform
You are My workmanship, not your own; I will reform
Living by the flesh, you will die, My Spirit transforms
I designed you, and I alone understand your human form

## January 2

## Think Service

**Revelation 5:13**

*And every creature which is in heaven, and on the earth, and under the earth, and such as are in the sea, and all that are in them, heard I saying, Blessing, and honour, and glory, and power, be unto him that sitteth upon the throne, and unto the Lamb for ever and ever.*

Fear not, for I Am the Lord your God, triumph in the year ahead
I will never forsake you; in My Presence, there's nothing to dread
Past troubles, sorrows, disappointments, I will cut off their thread
If you hold on to despair, heartaches, and pain; you will get misled

Dwell only on My daily gift to you; that's why it's called the present
Look how My beautiful creation absorbs My light, and it is content
*You* are My image and glory; for *you*, My Son made an investment
I guarantee your trust in Me is not in vain; that is My commitment

Remember His Resurrection as you arise each morning and rejoice
Discard all fear for you and your loved ones; think only of service
Failure, shortfall, despair, ill will, or gloom is not to be your choice
Eliminate all your anxiety, rely on Me every day, listen to My voice

My forgiveness ends the fear of sin you have spun; My Love is robust
Every new year is in My hands; as it unfolds day by day, I will adjust
Think confidently; My supply for each day is sure; know that I Am just
Yours is a risen life; prove it to Me by showing Me that you have trust

Fear breeds if you dwell on anxious thoughts about what lies ahead
Trust Me for the wisdom and strength you need to overcome instead
Come to Me all you who hunger and thirst, for I Am the living bread
As the disciples learned, pray to your heavenly Father, and be blessed

Do not let your quest for success mislead you; run to Me your prize
I love to discuss all your ideas, but tearing into the future is not wise
Have no doubt I Am your exceeding great reward, the best enterprise
Every sin you fall into, I will forgive; you cannot give Me a surprise

## January 3

## Help and Save

**Jeremiah 32:27**

*Behold, I Am the Lord, the God of all flesh: is there any thing too hard for me?*

You are not on earth just for yourself; you are here to help and save
Every day is a chance to share My love and help someone be brave
Past and Present and Future, I'll manage until we meet face to face
But you must keep trusting as you are running till you finish the race

The joy of your Lord is no ordinary joy; it is the singular gift that I fill
When you smile, when you love and serve, it gives Me such a thrill
You may not see Me, but I'm always there, doting as you do My will
Live your life always knowing, no matter when or where, only I fulfill

A sea of sin surrounds you; lift another out from doubt and despair
Fishers of men I call do not fear; for the Tempter is in My crosshairs
So lead doubters to faith, to courage, and have no qualms; I Am there

Rearrange your priorities, if necessary, your lifestyle change and share

I don't call you to a life of pleasure and glee but to keep Me in sight
Love and laugh as you strive; My yoke is easy, and My burden light
Onward My trusted child, remember it's by My Spirit, not by might
There is no room for gloom, but Trust, Love and Joy, your birthright!

When the going gets tough, I Am with you; I Am ready to sustain you
You can never fall outside of My reach, never, no matter what you do
Even if your sins cross the line unseen in death's vale, I come to rescue
Repent, look away from yourself and see how many lives can we renew?

## January 4

## I Will Make a Way

**Isaiah 40:31**
*But they that wait upon the Lord shall renew their strength; they shall mount up with wings as eagles; they shall run, and not be weary; and they shall walk, and not faint.*

I Am your Lord; I will renew and remake you, fear not
How precious you are to Me; you are in My every thought
I unleash all My love and mercy for you like a juggernaut
Think over this often, for you, was My salvation wrought

If you spread My love, it becomes the conquering force
Depend on Me for everything; know that I Am your source
Rest and let My Spirit flow; your painful past is no ghost!
Be of good cheer; there is a plan; My love will reinforce

You cannot enter My Kingdom unless you become a child
I created you to explore, in joy, live, laugh, and be wild!
How can you be fearful? I died to vindicate and reconcile
My children, know you are free; in Me, you're undefiled!

# January 5

## My Plan Will Unfold

**John 14:6**
*Jesus saith unto him, I Am the way, the truth, and the life: no man cometh unto the Father, but by me.*

Tell yourself often that in My kingdom, all is well
Every doubt, every fret, every care, you can repel
Full provision made for you in My ark, no alarm bells!
Living daily in My presence is being safe in a citadel

So don't plan as people of the world do and dread
They doubt they can trust Me for their daily bread
Foolishly carry heavy loads I can substitute instead
Tell of your Great Burden-Bearer; to people misled

Do not let the future worry; every step will unfold
Nothing happens to you outside My will in My hold
Provision comes with a guarantee in My household
One day's share for you is more than enough to hold

## January 6

## Lack Is Nothing

**Isaiah 43:1**
*Fear not: for I have redeemed thee, I have called thee by thy name; thou art mine.*

No evil can befall you when you remain in My will
Do not fall prey to imaginary angst making you ill
Just get a grip on My love, and you know the thrill!
Rest, take no thought for tomorrow; watch me fulfill

In My company, peace like a river flows so quietly
It passes all understanding; and is yours constantly
Reassuring, cleansing, and fulfilling desires perfectly
Burdens get lifted, confidence is restored permanently

Start and end your day with Me; in a time set aside
I cherish your devotion, and I will be there to abide
You may not sense My Presence always; I may hide
Don't give up on our huddles; I Am there. I Am beside

Evil spirits cannot enter; pay no heed to the Doubter
You are mine, protected; if you know Me, your Master
Tired nerves, failing hope, doubts, and sins no matter
Nothing should you fear; I've conquered the Monster

Hoard nothing, do not fear money, let it flow in and out
A time of lack is nothing more than a necessary workout
Faith like a mustard seed is enough; just don't burnout
My provision for you is not something that fades out

## January 7

### Like a War-Horse

**James 1:17**
*Every good gift and every perfect gift is from above,*
*and cometh down from the Father of lights, with whom*
*is no variableness, neither shadow of turning.*

Your heavenly Father cares for you; He is always alert
Watch, He will make a way; your prayers do not divert
His plans will unfold; in loving you, God is no introvert!
Every door He will open; evil has no power to subvert

Have you reason to fear? Hasn't God proven His care?
Protected you and helped you escape from every snare?
Treasure My company, be serene in this time we share
Be regular; peace, calm, trust, and be sure of your prayer

Hide My Word in your heart and learn to keep a routine
It is not only a lamp unto your feet; it is true medicine
You are My precious instruments, be sharp in discipline
I've designed you with purpose like a fine-tuned engine

Ask of Me My Will, according to My Spirit—nothing amiss
I will respond to every flitting thought, your every wish
Your every deed I will employ, your defeats too, I cherish
My miracle-working power is yours; you will be astonished

But I have made My purity and virtue necessary for you
My power is entrusted only to a war-horse tried and true
When you are trained and fit, My potential shines through
You are ready when you know it is only Me you look up to

# January 8

## Nothing to Pay

**Luke 12:32**
*Fear not, little flock; for it is your Father's good pleasure to give you the kingdom.*

My gift of eternal life is an unimaginable forever stay
Incredible wonders unravel that you cannot see; pray
You stand upon the threshold of eternity, only obey
Because My Son redeems you, there is nothing to pay

You sing of a Silent Night when My Kingdom arrived
Unseen, it enters man's heart; it is the ultimate prize
Like the wind, it blows, its source unknown—disguised
Listen to Me quietly, often without a message retrieved

Your God speaks in a still, small voice, a silent soft wind
Each message steered for your heart; and so well-timed
My speech is rarely heard—direct interaction a rare find
But My Will, I do not hide, and I'll never leave you blind

Know your Bible; every Word of mine draws My people
Lead them to their Pearl of Great Price, as My disciple
You possess treasure men long for; give them a sample
Place it strategically into their hearts; it is entirely legal

I said, "Be, ye therefore perfect as your heavenly Father"
I don't ask you to "do" perfection, but "be"—My follower
Don't take a lifetime to grasp it; time flies; do not dither
Will you abide in Me to succeed? We can do it together

# January 9

## Don't Generalize

**Matthew 6:27**
*Which of you by taking thought can add one cubit unto his stature?*

My challenges can be rough, but they will make you wise
I do not shield you from hardships; My peace, I promise
Trust My loving care, but it's not something to generalize
Love is not always a mountaintop high; I do also chastise

What is joy but an intimate recognition of My will in it all
Trials and closed doors, none can ever be your downfall
Your afflictions work for you, preceding eternal windfall
Nothing gets wasted in My kingdom, there is no shortfall

## January 10

## Suffering Is Progress

**2 Corinthians 4:17**

*For our light affliction, which is but for a moment, worketh for us a far more exceeding and eternal weight of glory.*

Are you weighed down with burdens too heavy to carry?
Wrong choices overwhelm and seem increasingly scary
Haven't you heard My offer? All your burdens, I will ferry
Then why all the strain? Walk with Me; life can be merry!

Be calm, no matter what occurs, learn to be patient
Your Master fearfully crafted His fragile instrument
I know what you can bear in My loving chastisement
Suffering is progress, My one important assignment

I will never ask you to carry even one extra day's load
Are you serving another master, that two-horned toad?
Are stardom, man's applause, riches, and lust your gods?
You are weary, burdened; come to Me; I will not fraud

## January 11

## A New Reality

**1 John 2:25**
*And this is what he hath promised us, even eternal life.*

To all who have My gift of salvation, eternity has begun
Reality is immortality; everything will change one by one
You are an eternal being with a new existence you've won
Distinct forever life is yours, and My writ is never undone

See the spectacular dimension of a soul with life eternal
Understand your body and spirit ceased to be terminal
Ponder on the secrets of My Kingdom; they're personal
Your witness to men lasts forever; always be relational

## January 12

## Not a Cliché

**Psalm 46:10**
*Be still, and know that I Am God: I will be exalted among the heathen, I will be exalted in the earth.*

"Seek and you shall find" is a promise, not a mere cliche
Every humble cry gets My response; tears wiped away
Needs met, and access granted to My heavenly cache
The God-fearing are wise; they've learned how to pray

Think of life as a walk with Me on the road to Emmaus
I love to share meals with weary travelers in every house
Men often forget I Am at supper with the kids and spouse
Listening, observing, I watch a family, quiet as a mouse

If you seek Me, I Am always ready to walk the extra mile
My disciples didn't recognize Me, so I waited for a while
Till they did, then My Resurrection changed their lifestyle
Trust My Word; even a quiet walk with Me is never futile

You are the ones who didn't see yet you have believed
So did My mother; when God incarnated, she received
After My Ascension, My troubled disciples, perceived
Thomas quit doubting; Holy Spirit at Pentecost revealed

You, too, be confident I Am present, know I Am around
Your unseen Lord is more tangible than the solid ground
My Light is your very Life, in My radiant Love I surround
Seek Me with your whole heart, you'll live and settle down

I give you marching orders daily; you are pilgrims on patrol
Like Nehemiah, you receive all necessary to reach your goal
Delight in steady supply, know Jerusalem's road is no stroll
Till heaven's gate, My indwelling ecstasy, you do not know

Oh! Listen to Me joyously! let none distance you and Me
There is nobody out in the world, no one you need to see
I Am the terminator of death and sin; only I can set you free
Earthly rants pull, I draw back till you see My true reality

## January 13

## Seek Life

**Colossians 4:2**
*Continue in prayer, and watch in the same with thanksgiving.*

I Am the Lord, is anything too hard for Me—rejoice and progress!
Can you thank Me for everything, especially trials and distress?
Where you arrive at the place of joyful living; that's when I bless
It is an assignment you need to score high for managing stress

Your heavenly Father loves to see you content in ups and downs
Imparting biblical truths can help you and others in any meltdown
Share My Word with the needy; precious diamonds, theirs to own
People needlessly hurt, ignoring great truths that remain unknown

I long to hear each life and heart cry, "Come quickly, Lord Jesus."
But I know what is in man; the unrepentant won't reason or discuss
In My time on earth, the people wanted miracles crying, please us
Come to Me to seek life, not continue in bondage to that Octopus

## January 14

## Bring Others

**Romans 10:15**
*And how shall they preach, except they be sent? as it is written, How beautiful are the feet of them that preach the gospel of peace, and bring glad tidings of good things!*

You are a channel for My love; never lose hope, never surrender
Evil tries to overwhelm; you will conquer, I Am your defender
My Gethsemane desolation exposed the tools of the Pretender
Harness Calvary's clout to serve Me in Resurrection splendor!

No champion of mine would fall prey to evil if they could unveil
Satan's utter delight in every sinful collapse when men turn tail
The pain and setback of those who long for loved ones to prevail
Arise in My Name! Conquest awaits; evil together we will impale

Gold must go through the crucible, only tested until it is purified
You, My treasured instrument washed in My blood, are sanctified
Can you hear the drums, My warrior? Victory is yours, unqualified
Now tenderly, as a bold fisher of men, bring Me others to glorify

## January 15

## Self Must Die

**Romans 6:6**

*Knowing this, that our old man is crucified with him, that the body of sin might be destroyed, that henceforth we should not serve sin.*

Walk with Me on the road to Emmaus, and you are fortified
But one challenge is within to overcome, a great peril—pride
Extinguish *self*. Every blow to it shapes the true, eternal side
My Spirit is like unseen wind, My transformation doesn't hide

Don't compromise whenever *self* prods you to action but deny
Conquer all life challenges, when with *self* you refuse to comply
I trampled flesh to death; set your mind on things above to defy
Walk in My Spirit; freedom is yours, understand flesh must die

Pain will not overwhelm you; I know just how much you can bear
After Resurrection, I sent My disciples the Comforter to take care
Warned of suffering waiting ahead, had made them greatly scared
Ten would die, My Spirit-led martyrs, trusting in their Lord's prayer

You, too, may not understand; obey, walk, and listen to Me; you will
My revelations and teachings are all guaranteed to give you a thrill

You are My work in progress, be sure I will complete you with skill
It's not your striving as in running a race, but My purpose to fulfill

## January 16

### I Am Your Reality

**Psalm 118:5–6**

*I called upon the LORD in distress: the LORD answered me, and set me in a large place. The LORD is on my side; I will not fear: what can man do unto me?*

Newness, serenity, no tension, fearless and carefree
Your mistakes absolved for best outcomes, ultimately
In an uncertain world, learn poise, soul balance in Me
I Am your unchanging Maker; trust—I Am your reality

My power to cast out evil in men and women is all yours
Unapplied, you lose it; employ in continuous endeavors
Life altering work, it is not high pressure it surely restores
Have no fear, abide in My Power, know I have no failures

It's the same Power I used to cast out devils when on earth
Don't say you're too busy, rescuing souls is of great worth
Only, do not attempt this vital work without My new birth
Then led by My Spirit, renewed each time boldly go forth

## January 17

## Anchor My Love

**Colossians 3:23–24**

*And whatsoever ye do, do it heartily, as to the Lord, and not unto men; Knowing that of the Lord ye shall receive the reward of the Inheritance: for ye serve the Lord Christ.*

Daily strivings count, not just heights you climb infrequently
Obey My Will in dreary desert or mountaintop, persistently
Endurance in your spiritual life is what's needed consistently
Humdrum Kingdom assignments teach you essential humility

Life is a patchwork quilt; every stitch can complete My design
No contribution is too small; everything you do, I can enshrine
Be like a bricklayer building a cathedral; a labor of love, genuine
I know a day-to-day grind is no small feat, and I Am your lifeline

Do you wonder what I expect as you engage in your daily fray?
I love to see you take a break, relax, and find time to slip away
You sense My joy; you try to figure it out, and you want to pray
Shed religiosity; come as you are; My love is the only gateway

Your Lord cares about the little things; your work plays a part
In My vast creation scheme, every little stone is a piece of art
Failure doesn't matter; people do, everyone gets a fresh start
Joy in Me and anchor My love; remember, I've set you apart

## January 18

## I Will Deliver

**Psalm 18:2**

*The LORD is my rock, and my fortress, and my deliverer; my God, my strength, in whom I will trust; my buckler, and the horn of my salvation, and my high tower.*

Imperfection can dare to rely on My perfection; there's no debate
Silence is golden in My presence; seek Me *first*, then trust and wait
Abide in Me; it's that simple, I love you, I understand, and I relate
That's your part; mine is to hem you in, where no evil can penetrate

Your attitude counts; love in action, in witness to all My needy ones
All humanity must have salvation; I died to bring to glory many sons
As My channels, Sowers of My Word; use the power of your tongues
Time is short, unbelief is growing, many today call themselves nones

Your needs supplied, in good measure, pressed down, running over
Trust My divine indulgence; I long to provide generously whatever
Combat your worries; allow no impatience, trust; I Am your Provider

Physical, emotional, psychological, or spiritual needs, I will
deliver

My love and trust dissolve worries and cares you may conceive
Fretting and fuming, anxiety can erode your stability and
deceive
They take you beyond help if you lose sight of Me and disbelieve
Prevail and persevere; you'll never lose heart if, to Me, you
cleave

## January 19

## I Am Reality

**Psalm 139:7–8**
*Whither shall I go from thy spirit? or whither shall I flee from thy presence? If I ascend up into heaven, thou art there: if I make my bed in hell, behold, thou art there.*

True faith is My faithfulness; trust is My trueness; I Am Reality
Faithlessness dislodges Me, but seekers will gain indemnity
Ask for the gift of Faith to be fruitful; that is your responsibility
It is your primary need to achieve an exceptional productivity

Work is worship undergirded by prayer, not motivated by greed
You have to work, you have to pray, and trust I meet your need
What is Faith without fruit? Pray it flourishes like a mustard seed
For it is the required weapon you must have if you are to succeed

To overcome evil, every adverse situation, and accomplish good
Faith is the envelope to send Me your request in every likelihood
"Faith without works is dead." A combination not fully understood
Trusting Me is all you need; I will empower you in My parenthood

## January 20

## My Love Foresees

*James 4:3*
*Ye ask, and receive not, because ye ask amiss, that ye may consume it upon your lusts.*

I will never confound anyone who believes in Me
Long before you share a need, I receive your plea
Before you even figure things out, I have foreseen
For only I know what the best for you should be

Like a loving parent preparing for their child's future
Daughter or son, I'm ready for your every adventure
Marriage, college, job, or undertaking, even a failure
Be sure of My love, fear not, no matter what venture

My love anticipates, but My people don't remember
You wail and plead in supplication as if I encumber
Forgetting your God is Love; for you, I do not slumber
My treasure is yours; come as you are, not as a briber

Petitioning Me with lament and whimpering is not Faith
Be a rebel, seize your inheritance, boldly enter My gate
What a delight it is to see you inquire about your estate
Confident, knowing you are a citizen, not an expatriate

Where did your parents learn to love you if not from Me?
Father, Son, and Holy Spirit, the source of love, the Trinity
Giving you gifts is our joy, eternal love, your opportunity
Heaven rejoices when My truth frees you for immortality

## January 21

## On Things Above

**Ephesians 4:5–6**
*One Lord, one faith, one baptism, One God and Father of all, who is above all, and through all, and in you all.*

One with Father, Son, and Spirit. One in the Lord of infinity!
Could any human aspiration transcend union in the Trinity?
In such authority, only think, and thought animates into equity
Set your affections on things above, not on things of mortality

You are a mystery; the garment of flesh is not your real identity
Dwell on the material when living in Me, and you create reality
Be careful then; desire profit, not detriment, to your spirituality
In the spiritual arena, the law will replicate in a similar capacity

Think *Love,* and Love will gird all whom you cherish or consider
Think *ill will* and offense provokes, for vexation it will engender
Think well-being—good health will invigorate you, not hinder
The physical mirrors the mental and spiritual; it's like a blender

## January 22

## Chat Anywhere

**Psalm 145:18–19**
*The LORD is nigh unto all them that call upon him, to all that call upon him in truth. He will fulfil the desire of them that fear him: he also will hear their cry, and will save them.*

I send forth My Spirit to create, and the earth I restore
When My Word goes out, against it no power can endure
Calmly go about your day; with nothing to fear anymore
Facing challenges with praise songs, give Me an encore

Ceaseless prayer is not a bore; it's a cozy chat anywhere
Take love as your cue, your gladness and rejoicing share
Rest joyfully; I Am there; I have all the time for your care
I haven't given you a spirit of fear, and nothing can scare

## January 23

## Be Thankful

**Proverbs 6:23**
*For the commandment is a lamp; and the law is light; and reproofs of instruction are the way of life.*

Your Lord's hand is not too short to save, but I Am no enforcer
Why are you afraid? Aren't I your God and Deliverer? Answer!
Could it be you are unsure, and hence a "sitting on the fencer"?
Indeed, I say, believe Me for eternal life; I Am your Savior

Your hope is unseen, but Faith in Me is salvation's guarantee
Only, not *your* faith, My credibility; not *your* trust, My reality
On the gloomiest days, never stop trusting Me—thankfully
Practice this on gray days; you will experience My reliability

At Calvary, I trampled death by death to redeem My world
My Last Supper, Passion, Death, and Resurrection unfurled
Training for all My followers—serving in a brave new world
Only one of My Apostles, John, survived where they labored

If on any gray day you are not thankful, the lesson will repeat
Only for those who seek to serve Me even in failure or defeat
Those can come with each assignment, but you cannot retreat
Every Faith work receives My anointing by the Holy Paraclete

## January 24

## I Entrust Power

**Psalm 46:1**
*God is our refuge and strength, a very present help in trouble.*

All power in heaven and earth is given to Me by My Father
Dwelling in Me, you naturally receive; so, you take it further
Live in My Presence and obtain; My gifts are yours to gather
Courage, Wisdom, Joy, Provision I entrust to My co-worker

Doesn't My Word reassure? I have not given you a spirit of fear
But of Power, Love, and a Sound Mind; ponder on them, be clear
What more do you need? You don't see Me, but I Am always near
Hagar called Me El Roi, "The God who sees me." So, persevere

## January 25

## Coin in a Fish

**Matthew 6:33**
*But seek ye first the kingdom of God, and his righteousness; and all these things shall be added unto you.*

Pray for Faith; you must but for those who abide yet are faint
I understand human weakness; I've been there, no complaint
Rely on Me for help when in need; fear cannot crush My saint
It's merely "False Evidence Appearing Real"—the devil's feint

When I Am your Guide, you don't need to see the road ahead
Sufficient for one day is evil's foray; you count on Me instead
I seldom permit a view of your future on the road you tread
One step at a time is My way to cultivate Faith with no dread

God of the Universe, I was confined to human limitations
You must learn spiritual vision and power need formation
In temporal affairs, you too must submit to My restrictions
I Am always there. Peter fished out a coin for tax, no tension

In uncharted waters, the Lord of the oceans is by your side
Controlling storms as you sing for joy, watching Me, mystified
In pure freedom, serve your God, the seas obey, He who decides
I Am your calm, all-powerful, forthright, and kind Jesus, abide

## January 26

## Shelter in My Love

**2 Corinthians 9:8**
*And God is able to make all grace abound toward you; that ye, always having all sufficiency in all things, may abound to every good work.*

Consummating your life to God ensures real peace and joy
The base and bedrock of our intimacy; nothing can destroy
In My Father's house are many mansions for you to enjoy
For happiness on earth, too, it's a promise you can employ

The pact applies for here and now, eternity, the great bounty
I designed life on earth for abundance, not something chintzy
It becomes a hopeless struggle only outside My sovereignty
A product abused violates a warranty, revokes the guarantee

Obedience brings you understanding, insight, vision, and cheer
Peace is yours, passing all understanding, and you lose all fear
My plans for you are astonishing—if you only obey and adhere
Shelter in My love, protection, and freedom, and you persevere

## January 27

## Nothing Can Alarm

**John 14:27**

*Peace I leave with you, my peace I give unto you: not as the world giveth, give I unto you. Let not your heart be troubled, neither let it be afraid.*

When your Spirit-Life is true, it's unruffled; nothing can alarm
Trust all to Me; it's a challenge; stay serene, and fear no harm
Not disturbed or distracted, not even for a moment, all is calm
Will you doubt years of blessing because of a fleeting storm?

Regardless of *who* or *what,* your task is to block the incursion
My Power diverts into other channels, do not allow depression
Pour out your blessings, and I will bless you with more unction
Share My grace in abundance when you receive a benediction

My Power must flow; every blessing must reach the uninitiated
It doesn't matter even if you come across people uninterested
Practice how to be a blessing every day, how to get connected
Abide and dwell in My Presence; I love to meet you unexpected

## January 28

## In the Tempest

**Psalm 118:6**
*The LORD is on my side; I will not fear: what can man do unto me?*

Go forward unafraid in health and strength, peace all 365 days
Happiness and joy—they are all My gifts; ask Me for the ways
The spiritual and material worlds hold no empty places to stay
If self and fears depart, the Spirit you crave will take His place

My Father is a Father to you, sons, and daughters, so blessed
You love and guard your children, at your Father God's behest
God is love; hold that thought, imagine His passion and interest
Numbered is every hair on your head; do not fear the tempest!

I waited to rescue My apostles until the storm was at its peak
Amidst their panic, I napped in their boat; I knew it could leak
That's My training for brave souls; I want you strong but meek
Calming your storms, for the first gust of wind leaves you weak

So let the terrors come; nothing can harm when I Am there
It is okay to lose your nerve; My disciples felt I didn't care
Gently convicted of My protection when they became aware
Joyfully anticipate My intervention, in your worst nightmare

## January 29

## My Great Plan

**Psalm 32:8**
*I will instruct thee and teach thee in the way which thou shalt go: I will guide thee with mine eye.*

Do not flinch at being busy; I call for sacrifice and service
To be the greatest in My kingdom, labor without prejudice
My disciples had to learn, and so do you, as My apprentice
I serve the humblest, the lowliest, all who need My justice

Succor one and all, seek out the needy, making no distinction
Make imparting the best, not gain, be your one preoccupation
Faithfully following Me can often call for a complete reversion
But your turnaround will lead to a marvelous transformation

Read the morning daily, watch the news, and what do you find?
Men favor no holds barred competitions; why do they spellbind?
Do man's earthly aims, and ambitions bring him peace of mind?
Name, fame, honor, wealth, deceive, freedom they mostly bind

And yet, to men who listen, above the world's din, there rings
2000 years of My message, My gentle continuous pleadings
Come to Me, you weary and heavy laden, for rest and blessing
If the lost turn, they find their calm and a heart full of singing

Health to the Sick, Wealth to the Poor, Food to the Hungry, I Am
Home to Wanderers, Rapture to Jaded, Love to the Lonely, I Am
Not *one* want of the soul, do I not supply for the asking, for man
I long to be all for all—how can I not be? That is My great plan

## January 30

## I Will Satisfy

**Jeremiah 18:6**
*O house of Israel, cannot I do with you as this potter?*
*Saith the LORD. Behold, as the clay is in the potter's hand,*
*so are ye in mine hand, O house of Israel.*

The future is in My sight; I know men's longings to satisfy
Know all is well; outside My Will for you, none can apply
Rely on Me; you are not at the mercy of fate or another guy
I will remove anything against your purpose if not an ally

Never fear, don't try to plan; I Am the Potter crafting My clay
I have told you what is good, what I require of you every day
Do justice, love goodness, walk humbly with your God, pray
When you face the worst, My grace abounds; I do not delay

Be rooted and grounded in Me, Christ—the Rock, your base
My Divinity is the Corner Stone, your firm foundation in place
Simply depend on Me for everything—nothing can disgrace
His evil forgiven, David took after My own heart—My ace

## January 31

## I Make Good

**1 Peter 5:10**
*But the God of all grace, who hath called us unto his eternal glory by Christ Jesus, after that ye have suffered a while, make you perfect, establish, strengthen, settle you.*

In My care, no evil can befall; the slavery of Joseph I made good
Naomi and Ruth's misfortune turned to profit despite widowhood
Rahab, harlot of Jericho, I justified; in My lineage is her sainthood
I chose you, called you out of darkness into My royal priesthood

Retreat often into My presence; know that I Am your hiding place
Time with Me is restoration, power, and peace in a healing space
Plan dates to unwind with Me now and then—quiet days of grace
Awaken refreshed—to physically, mentally, spiritually resurface

In My service, you will never carry a burden you cannot bear
My plans exceed your highest hopes for your rest and welfare
Your security, guidance, and success are My priority, and care
Harbor no thoughts of self, My love, joy, peace you must share

My gifts cover needs on the physical, mental, and spiritual plane
Favors that hide wonder, working attributes for your every gain
If your inner life is all it should be, then My work will fully attain
Not in the rat race, but in the battle for your soul, you will reign

# February

## February 1

## No Needless Suffering

**Psalm 34:19**
*Many are the afflictions of the righteous: but the LORD delivereth him out of them all.*

I have built sacrifice and suffering in My redemption plan
Be willing to be used and to help uplift your fellow man
It is not by mere chance that I called you to be a fisherman
All humanity needs My salvation; you must understand

Lack not in zeal; serve faithfully, steward God's grace
I redeemed My world, but men choose to sin as slaves
As the heavens are higher, so are My thoughts, My ways
Emptying myself, I took the form of a servant to save

You are to go; therefore, make disciples in every nation
Tell of repentance and forgiveness of sins to My creation
Everyone who calls upon My name is freed and forgiven
Your Lord of the harvest needs laborers to fill positions

## February 2

## Eternal Youth

**John 4:35**
*Say not ye, There are yet four months, and then cometh harvest? behold, I say unto you, Lift up your eyes, and look on the fields; for they are white already to harvest.*

Take courage and give someone a glimpse of Me today
Start their journey from the mind to the heart, don't delay
They must seek Me in truth for My kingdom, the only way
Curiosity about faith without change is mere religious play

Tell about your Savior, though many refuse to take part
Never mind, some will think it over; you may light a spark
Something vital will start stirring deep inside their heart
New life in Me begins when anyone hears, makes a start

What brings someone to Faith in Me or keeps them aloof?
Religious tradition can hinder. Is your witness bulletproof?
Does your life prove you separated falsehood from the truth?
You claim to know Me; are you authentic under your roof?

I redeemed all at Calvary; how can people be disinterested?
My salvation is free, yet many scorn the freedom I granted
Heaven's doors are open; those who won't enter are subverted
Tell them of My love; for in their liberation, I remain invested

If the unbelieving oppose My Holy Spirit; they choose untruth
Life passes away for *all*, but in Me, *all* resurrect to eternal youth
And I Am partial to none; in My lineage, I have Rahab and Ruth
My greatest joy is when all My children return and rise in Truth

## February 3

## The Greatest Lesson

**John 4:10–11**

*Herein is love, not that we loved God, but that he loved us, and sent his*
*Son to be the propitiation for our sins. Beloved, if God so loved us,*
*We ought also to love one another.*

Why would people need a Savior if I came only for the righteous?
You too must Love all the difficult people, your efforts tenacious
Make it habitual; practice until loving everyone becomes continuous
Nothing impossible in My power, even if winning souls is dangerous

Without love, you cannot dwell in Me; it's the greatest lesson I preach
Those who don't Love don't know I Am Love; to every sinner, I beseech
Only if you have Love can you know God, learn to love all, and outreach
I created you in Love to share My redeeming love whenever you go teach

## February 4

## The Treasure Map

**1 Corinthians 2:5**
*That your faith should not stand in the wisdom of men, but in the power of God.*

Be strong. Take courage in your heart; fear not; new life awaits
Why are you so anxious all the time? I long for you to appreciate
Human life is a treasure map; it only appears as an obstacle race
I designed every lap for you; take each in your stride in My grace

Run at a steady pace, discover every hidden treasure one by one
Life is a test of endurance; add worry, and it's harder to get done
All grateful hearts I bless; My eternal award is awaiting everyone
Believe in Me for your marathon to freedom—do not be outdone

I take your Faith and add My Power—the nuts and bolts required
But you point to a few obstacles in your way; you are bewildered
You lack the certainty of My presence; you are fearful, uninspired
I test your endurance even as I manage every hurdle I've ordered

Why did the walls of Jericho fall? Not by might nor by power
Could it have happened if My people withdrew like cowards?
Shouts of Praise and obedience to My commands empowered
Every wall will collapse; against you, no weapon can prosper

If any human opposition prevails, I permit it for a time to assess
Watching it stand against you, I see you overcome, and I bless
When monarch's hearts are in My fist, how can you be so restless
Be sure of My rule and dominion; I will never leave you in distress

## February 5

## Remain in Me

**1 John 2:28**
*And now, little children, abide in him; that, when he shall appear, we may have confidence, and not be ashamed before him at His coming.*

I reveal My will step by step but rely on Me, not on another
Try it; you will be content, at Peace, and trusting, altogether
When you learn to count on Me alone, then you will discover
Family and friends may forsake you; I Am your sure armor

Just simple, authentic trust in Me; triggers My intervention
When you don't depend on anyone; that is My only condition
If you won't let go of your crutch, there is no transformation
My power is enough to help you overcome every limitation

I say remain in Me, and so many think that is being passive
Staying in Me is not inactive but combatting the corrosive
It resists the lie I only value you for something substantive
Trust Me for rest and provision; My supply is comprehensive

Remaining is trusting you'll have enough, and you *are* enough
Don't obsess about "making it," accumulating so much stuff
To overcome your scarcity thinking, learn how to get tough
Share what you have generously; hoarding makes life rough

Practice the rhythms of quiet rest and stillness; undeterred
The unsustainable lifestyle exhausts you, so heed My Word
Come to Me all ye who are weary; rest in your One Shepherd
I'll help you conquer the hurry and scurry of life; I'll undergird

## February 6

## Always Seek

**1 Chronicles 22:19**
*Now set your heart and your soul to seek the Lord your God.*

Walk with Me to learn. Listen to Me to hear Me speak
Come, despite every hurdle or resistance at its peak
Even on days I don't connect, in heart-to-heart speech
Persevere; make it a life habit; you must always seek

I reveal My will in beautiful ways, present and future
If you meet Me faithfully, I will share in your adventure
Of all life's tutors, few experience My close encounters
Every trial in life, can anyone explain but your Savior?

## February 7

## Longing for You

**Exodus 19:5**

*Now therefore, if ye will obey my voice indeed, and keep my covenant, then ye shall be a peculiar treasure unto me above all people: for all the earth is mine.*

Life's valleys and mountains teach it's not always upbeat
You won't feel My presence all the time. I can be discreet
Those who listen will hear Me; with seeking hearts, I meet
But know I Am with you; time with Me you must not forfeit

Eager multitudes would throng Me when I walked the earth
For healing, My teaching, or food, many uncaring of My worth
My creation, I came unto My own, but they gave Me no berth
Given free will, not all want to become sons of God in rebirth

As I met their needs, intervened, and saved, I longed to find
Amidst the crush, anyone who came to be near Me, so inclined
To seek Me, expecting nothing, a companion being of one mind
Love is My essence; be with Me sometimes. Will you be so kind?

Delight Me, stay awhile in My presence; make the time, pay a visit
As much as I long to see you regularly, you need to make it a habit
Come not for material needs, not even a message from the pulpit
I often went early to My Father to pray, do the same and inherit

Would you seek Me for nothing, like you spend time with a friend?
To be together, no agenda, the joy of camaraderie is your only end
Who designed love and longing in the human heart to inter-depend?
Yearning for My creation My loving heart exalts doesn't condescend

## February 8

## Faith or Farce?

**James 1:6**
*But let him ask in faith, nothing wavering. For he that wavereth is like a wave of the sea driven with the wind and tossed.*

Besetting sin must end; Faith is a farce if you *act* devout
Often, suffering is self-inflicted; repentance is the route
You, too, once walked in darkness with fear and doubt
Your heart cries caught My ears, and I checked them out

Creation's awe inspires faith, not dread, in My followers
Be childlike in trusting Me; shun all fears for My wonders
My power is yours, if you learn and harness it as partners
Paradise was the original plan for My sons and daughters

Eden awaits; fear not when life's journey nears completion
Boldly take the few steps remaining, with My confirmation
I conquered sin and death; now, focus on My grace application
Guide the fearful to Me, be faithful in My Great Commission

My followers know that their prayers are like a boomerang
When they arrive at heaven's doors, they don't simply hang
They return an answer; God listens, knowing every lifespan
Before your mother's womb, He knows when your life began

Human frailty is why I died for all; My Father understands
Know that God's will is the salvation of all; it's His one plan
Prayers He answers in many ways, but He is not a yes man
Trusting hearts know *how* God hears; for none does He ban

## February 9

## All Your Tension

**Deuteronomy 7:9**
*Know therefore that the LORD thy God, he is God, the faithful God, which keepeth covenant and mercy with them that love him and keep his commandments to a thousand generations.*

I Am Jehovah Jireh, your reliable supply; trust My provision
Bank on Me; have no fear; look only for My divine allocation
I do not forget; I will satisfy you and remove all your tension
But now and then, I may test your faith before My intervention

Testing is essential to work in My vineyard; I must authenticate
Great undertakings for Me; I evaluate and assign after I validate
The heavenly host celebrates when I ordain the right candidate
But My disciples must wait to start until My command to initiate

Depend on no one but Me; no human being can meet your need
I Am your defense and your one redemption that is guaranteed
When I try you, be patient, and wait upon your Lord, I will exceed
Fear not; from every failure, every sorrow; your freedom I decreed

I know what you need even before you do; let Me make it very clear
You are My inheritance; how can you fret knowing I Am your Savior?
Take possession of your being, be poised and always in good cheer
A crown of righteousness waits for all whose love for Me is sincere

## February 10

## Heart to Heart

**Job 33:14**
*For God speaketh once, yea twice, yet man perceiveth it not.*

I may not always speak, but you will sense Me in your heart
Designed fearfully for your Maker, of My being, you are a part
We don't need words to chat; heart-to-heart is how I impart
Even if you disconnect, My faithfulness, nothing can thwart

## February 11

## My Life Flows

**Song of Solomon 2:11–12**
*For, lo, the winter is past, the rain is over and gone;*
*The flowers appear on the earth; the time of the singing*
*of birds is come, and the voice of the turtle is heard in our land.*

I Am your Savior from all cares, troubles, and sin's thrall
In all these situations, never lose sight: I Am your all in all
No calamity on earth can overwhelm; I Am above them all
I will draw you out of many waters; I Am your true windfall

Your soul's lifeline to God, Faith, and Power is a strong bond
I created you to withstand crushing pressure like a diamond
Your troubles cannot exceed My reach; they cannot go beyond
Never fear; to every attempt at conquering you, I will respond

Consider My creation in winter; I strip the trees of character
Yet in their dead branches secretly flows My life-giving nectar
Sap can be edible, but it's not all sweet to taste; it is also bitter
Then behold, Spring with its sunshine ushers in a glorious Easter!

New life comes as flowers bud; fruit trees blossom after pruning
Once bare of beauty, disfigured, gloomy, seemingly no meaning
Nonetheless, in all their stark desolation, they keep on standing
Learn lessons from nature; it is all My faithfulness she is staging

Remember, your God is a Master Gardener; His pruning is perfect
Your joy indicates a thankful heart communicating to Me in effect
And My life flows in you with such beautiful expression to connect
Rejoice always, never cease to trust Me for help, and I will protect

## February 12

## The Crucial Skill

**Psalm 27:14**
*Wait on the LORD: be of good courage, and he shall strengthen thine heart: wait, I say, on the LORD.*

I know the way ahead is difficult, but you must keep going
Waiting can be hard to do in life, but I designed it knowing
It is necessary till you know My will; it's My way of showing
In Love, do I gauge your Faith, and it is all a part of growing

To understand your discipleship, I assign the unyielding dint
I teach you to wait. The doing seems easy than a restful stint
Many impair their work for Me because they decide to sprint
Calm. Haste is not My Kingdom order; they don't get the hint

Learn to rest. I'll never push you beyond your spiritual stride
Sometimes you feel helpless, adrift in the sea with no guide
The disciples were frantic in their boat in Galilee, so terrified
My walking on water miracle was for you, too, quietly abide

When you do, you will accomplish what you desire in My will
Your labor is never in vain but relying on Me is the crucial skill
Without Me, you can do nothing; working with Me is the thrill
But you must never fear; first discern, trust, and learn the drill

## February 13

## I Am Life

**Proverbs 8:35**
*For whoso findeth me findeth life, and shall obtain favour of the Lord.*

Joy is elusive if you do not discern the Truth; *I Am Life*
Constantly abide in Me; you overcome pain and strife
Forget Me, and frustration, worry, fear of the future rife
Rebirth is in Me; I Am your only foundation for new life

Root yourself in Me, and I will fill your consciousness
Do not yield; stay alert to My reality to have newness
In Me is fullness of joy; trust Me for your true success
Share situations, actions, and aims with Me to progress

Knowing Me and My Son Jesus whom I sent is Life Eternal
Be fully conscious of Me always; Faith cannot be nominal
Lukewarm belief creates a conviction unreal and terminal
The Life of the Ages is Spirit-led in My love and relational

## February 14

## Alongside You

**Hebrews 12:1**

*Wherefore seeing we also are compassed about with so great a cloud of witnesses, let us lay aside every weight, and the sin which doth so easily beset us, and let us run with patience the race that is set before us.*

When a runner sprints into a race, he has no concern for pain
In a marathon, the distance does not deter him; he runs to gain
But sighting the goal, every fiber of his being will exert and strain
Stamina will stretch beyond limits; his strength explodes to attain

Your goal is in sight; your race nears the finish, but one part awaits
I Am the Lord your strength; run with Me before the race terminates
With feet like that of a deer, the heights are yours; I will accelerate
Victory is sure; I Am alongside, take courage My child, concentrate

Heaven's archives record tales of many who abandoned their race
They started strong, but sighting the goal; they couldn't keep pace

The heavenly host pleaded for one last spurt, a cry for God's grace
But losing sight of Me, even close to the finish, they lost their place

Those are the saddest reports found in the catalogues of heaven
Of My people who scorned Me in the race of life, though forgiven
The Cross is foolishness to these runners who choose a life driven
By a cruel Taskmaster who, in the end, cannot deliver, it is proven

## February 15

## Mysterious Influence

**Matthew 6:6**
*But thou, when thou prayest, enter into thy closet, and when thou hast shut thy door, pray to thy Father which is in secret; and thy Father which seeth in secret shall reward thee openly.*

Your quiet time with Me is essential; it is how I can daily restore
Troubles overcome so many because My company, they ignore
Faith comes by hearing My Word; making you abide in Me more
In My presence is fullness of joy, strength, and healing in store

Men do not understand how time spent with Me is therapeutic
People indulge in substance abuse; many hooked on narcotics
To overcome their suffering or get high, they seek the ecstatic
Only change to My likeness, physically, spiritually, is authentic

I could heal My poor, sick world if people waited on Me daily
Whatever your sins may be, come, you never lose My intimacy
Remember, even I, a great while before day, prayed solitarily
Time invested with Me has influenced many souls mysteriously

For now, focus on your labor of love; if without one, search
I need cheerful workers in My vineyard, so do some research
To find work you love, take a risk for a more rewarding perch
Work is worship; if you don't love what you do, you will lurch

Work ceaselessly for the present; labor is appointed to you fairly
Every thought, action, prayer, yearning of your heart, offer daily
I want you to be humble before your God, love justice, and mercy
There is nothing more significant; than learning time with Me

## February 16

## Inspiration vs Ambition

**Acts 1:8**
*But ye shall receive power, after that the Holy Ghost is come upon you:*
*and ye shall be witnesses unto me both in Jerusalem, and in all Judaea,*
*and in Samaria, and unto the uttermost part of the earth.*

The Divine writ is enough for every life purpose and human need
But we must work together in this endeavor for men to get freed
Selfless helpers and My Divine power can change the world indeed
My Great Commission needs men and women who surrender greed

Knowing the difference between inspiration and ambition is vital
One comes from Me, the other from the one whose grip is fatal
Inspired people will always have enough work; it is not accidental
Joblessness could end if everyone understood this basic principle

## February 17

## Unflinching, Unshaken

**Deuteronomy 4:31**

*For the LORD thy God is a merciful God; he will not forsake thee, neither destroy thee, nor forget the covenant of thy fathers which he sware unto them.*

In meditation, you learn that your Spirit and I often converse
You may never hear My voice in the time we spend in discourse
Inhale My presence like fresh cool air, pure profit in your purse
In stillness and calm trust My supply, every blessing I disperse

I long to see when in Faith you stand firm, unflinching, unshaken
Whatever happens, you know I Am there, scorning fear, not taken
So many lack trust in My presence; they do not learn this lesson
In life's hustle, bustle, and turmoil, be still; I will never abandon

## February 18

## My Objective

**Isaiah 37:16**
*O LORD of hosts, God of Israel, that dwellest between the cherubims,*
*thou art the God, even thou alone, of all the kingdoms of the earth:*
*thou hast made heaven and earth.*

Occult powers have nothing to do with the spiritual; walk away
Spiritual revelation is never in the sensual; it's not the gateway
Woe to those who call evil good and good evil; you keep away
From any practicing sorcery or divination, do not be led astray

But when you commune with Me, it is not to ask Me questions
You must come to refresh your soul; in Me is your rejuvenation
When you worship in Church, do not expect to find perfection
It is to be near to Me; nothing else counts, have no expectation

If I give you adversity or affliction, know they are gifts to receive
I Am the living Bread from heaven; I died for My people to live
To dust, you will return, but death no more can hold you captive
You are My inheritance; eternally being with you is My objective

## February 19

## My Responsibility

**2 Timothy 4:18**

*And the Lord shall deliver me from every evil work, and will preserve*
*me unto his heavenly kingdom: to whom be glory for ever and ever, Amen.*

It isn't what I reveal; it is My divine power filling you when we meet
Let nobody come in the way of our time together; nothing compete
My blessings for you are unfolding; trust Me; I Am preparing a feast
You may be frail, but I designed you; I know your every heartbeat

You think it's you who must face the brunt of a situation in adversity
But all you need is to connect with Me, not succumb to any calamity
How can you think I Am inaccessible when you are My responsibility
I order your life as I ensure the sunrise every morning in its continuity

You do not need to make frantic appeals for My urgent intervention
I love to see you calmly sharing what happened in your desperation

Imploring on knees isn't adoration; it pains to see you in that condition
I'd rather know you trust Me as your loving parent, sharing information

## February 20

## My Repose

**Acts 17:28**

*For in him we live, and move, and have our being; as certain also of your own poets have said, For we are also his offspring.*

Meet every challenge with love and cheer, knowing I Am there
Oh! Do not fail Me in the last lap; it's at the finish; you cannot err
Every step of the way, your Lord runs alongside; you are My heir
Prayers go unanswered because someone gives up, doesn't dare

My child, never feel abandoned, and do not act for yourself in fear
Abide till the end; it's never too late; I Am invisible but very near
What does it mean if you lose hope? Think My Word is insincere?
But I have called you to endure to the end; I've made it very clear

Can you hold out to the finish? Run the race, fight the good fight
Audaciously, loving and laughing, engaging all odds in My might
Oh! My child, am I pushing you too hard? You can be forthright!
Every cry for help reaches Me; I will intervene if you're not alright

I store My secret treasures; they are not for everyone, only those
Who do not hanker after gold and silver, who long for My repose

Study My Word carefully; in every detail, I've hidden My purpose
You will overcome and succeed; My Will for you none can oppose

My Kingdom is like the treasure found in a field, and kept buried
Where riches, spiritual, mental, even material, are tangible, carried
But in Me, you must live and move and have your being unwearied
With no spirit of fear but My Power and Joy and Peace guaranteed

## February 21

## My Chosen Best

**1 Timothy 6:17**

*Charge them that are rich in this world, that they be not high minded, nor trust in uncertain riches, but in the living God, who giveth us richly*
*all things to enjoy.*

I've destined you for success; pray and place before Me your requests
Notice in business, the owner and staff discuss all matters of interest
As My steward report to Me on payments, earnings etc., at My behest
But no need to beg; you aren't just My manager, but My chosen best

Lay all your matters before Me, and boldly expect immediate supply
Whatever is according to My will, I deliver; perhaps I'll even multiply
It is what I long to do, but I do test your Faith, see what is necessary
Help you grow till you learn I Am reliable; I may ask you to reapply

## February 22

## Let Me Minister

**John 14:18**
*I will not leave you comfortless: I will come to you.*

Do not strive to know the future; walk one step with Me daily
My Word is a lamp to your feet, the light guiding you steadily
Fear no calamity, why is your frail self succumbing to anxiety?
The restless soul is at risk, vulnerable to spiritual catastrophe

Spirit discord is to be feared, not a natural or self-inflicted disaster
A troubled heart casts a long shadow; not trusting your Commander
Come away to our meeting place for restoration, and let Me minister
When anxiety is great within you, just remember I Am your deliverer

Man's feeble will alone can thwart My divine power; no evil force can
You are at risk only when you lose sight of Me and fall prey to Satan
Predators take the stragglers on life's trail, all unsure of their Guardian
How can you ever feel abandoned? Courage! You are not an orphan!

Fearfully and wonderfully, I designed in you a free will to decide

Believe in the foolishness of the Cross or doubt with human pride
I know the hopeless reasonings of the wise, do not take their side
Fools mock My sacrifice for sin, but every cry of salvation I provide

## February 23

## My Ready Resources

**Matthew 6:34**

*Take therefore no thought for the morrow: for the morrow shall take thought for the things of itself. Sufficient unto the day is the evil thereof.*

If there is one lesson you must learn, it is to trust Me implicitly
Total confidence in Me if you want your Lord to lead constantly
Access to the Promised Land denied to My people proved costly
It was not My will; Israel's dread and disbelief barred their entry

For forty years, My people wandered in the desert, in doubt and fear
I parted the Red Sea; I mocked the terror and might of Egypt's spear
But My disobedient people scorned My Word, and they wouldn't hear
Will you also stubbornly choose the barren desert life year after year?

I died for your salvation from sin and all its debilitating consequences
But your doubts and worries can block the flow of My ready resources
Oh! If only you understood, I love you, regardless of the circumstances
What will it take to trust Me unconditionally and come to your senses?

## February 24

## My Restoring Love

**Proverbs 14:23**
*In all labour, there is profit: but the talk of the lips tendeth only to penury.*

Joy fills a life that stays busy; work is My precious gift, not a drudgery
You must try to find a labor of love or fill your labor with love eagerly
I've blessed you with talents, but finding profitable work is a discovery
Do not envy the success of others; find your niche and live productively

Enjoy the outdoors; My sunshine and fresh air bring you much healing
Stress, worries, and fears infect the body; your system needs cleaning
Inward joy transforms: purifies blood to flow with life-giving meaning
Body, Mind and Soul heal within, when My Spirit, My love is restoring

## February 25

## Remember Your Reprieve

**2 Timothy 2:24–25**

*And the servant of the Lord must not strive; but be gentle unto all men, apt to teach, patient, in meekness instructing those that oppose*
*themselves; if God peradventure will give them repentance to the acknowledging of the truth.*

You can sense My Spirit at work, but your life is resistant to change
Do not be discouraged by sin; My grace is sufficient for eternal gain
Your light and fleeting troubles will achieve an everlasting exchange
My child, you, I must renew; I am the same, but you were estranged

Cast your bread on many waters and give freely, having no regret
My blessings are to share and never to hoard; life's one big secret
I send angels in disguise, welcome them, love for all your magnet
I send unanticipated guests to test that your hospitality is well set

In My broken world, there is always someone needing a hand
Today they may rebuff you, but tomorrow, they will understand
Freely you have received, freely give in My name—no reprimand
Tell of their Savior who longs for them; it is My loving command

Let nobody ever feel rejected; every soul you must gladly receive
You will be amazed how things turn around if you genuinely believe
Don't hold back; give it your all; in My service, none can overachieve
The harvest is great, but My laborers few; remember your reprieve

## February 26

### Your One Quest

**1 John 5:11**

*And this is the record, that God hath given to us eternal life, and this life is in his Son.*

For peace, joy, and love, My hurting people need to understand
God's love, the world's most powerful source, is at your command
A love beyond any human bond, and still, so many misunderstand
Prodigal children, your heavenly Father waits; flee your wasteland

Develop a radical reliance on Divine Providence; you will be at rest
Do I have to repeat time and again that every difficulty is your test
When I declared, "It is finished," at the Cross, humanity, I blessed
Pray ceaselessly: Jesus, Jesus, Savior, Conqueror, your single quest

When your tears well up in distress, reach out for the balm of Gilead
That is symbolic of soothing and healing, but I Am the fountainhead
Do you fear poverty, ill health, loneliness, or failure? Trust Me instead!
Fake worries seem real; scorn them; calling My name will banish dread

Confront your fears with a joyful attitude that brooks no nagging doubt
My grace abounds when you fail, so bounce back from every knockout
No weapon set against you can prosper, nothing My Love cannot takeout
You can only fail if you do not believe I Am safeguarding you throughout

Every sin, every curse, every dread I conquered to save you at Calvary
For every human being, My offer of Redemption is their eternal sanctuary
But even a gift freely given must be rejected or received by a beneficiary
I designed you with free will to choose; receiving salvation is voluntary

## February 27

## Take a Holiday

**2 Corinthians 8:9**

*For ye know the grace of our Lord Jesus Christ, that, though he was rich, yet for your sakes he became poor, that ye through his poverty might be rich.*

Your lack comes from focusing on poverty when you are so rich
At your heavenly Father's banquet, will you only pick a sandwich?
Trust Me implicitly, and do not worry about every fleeting twitch
I own the world, don't bury your head in the sand like an ostrich

In the desert, a man will die of thirst if he cannot find any water
He must find the right source; if he doesn't, he can't be a survivor
You cannot thirst if I lead you in the wilderness as your Savior
I Am the aquifer, Life is in Me, do not go where there's no provider

As sure as you are, you will wake up in the morning to a new day
Can you not believe My help arrives on time? I will never delay
You trust friends to lend a hand; can I evade you when you pray?
A thousand years is like a day; I control time; so, rest and holiday!

I grieve to see the lack of Faith that instills so much fear in people
Learning to trust Me is your most vital lesson, and it is so simple

You can do nothing without Me; if you keep trying, it will cripple
I taught you to pray, share your heart as I do with every disciple

But what if I do not respond and the thing you fear comes to pass
A loved one dies, or a severe financial setback causes terrible loss
Will you lose Faith in Me? Will your anger make you deny the Cross?
I Am the Resurrection and the Life; trust Me to make good every loss

You must, however, take some time to evaluate and do an inventory
Did your money trouble arise for decisions biblically contradictory?
Do you mourn for any willful deviation from My life-giving trajectory?
I Am your blessed rest; there is no end when you come home to Me

## February 28

## Listen and Pray

**Matthew 8:5–6**

*And when Jesus was entered into Capernaum, there came unto him a centurion, beseeching him, the centurion answered and said, Lord, I Am not worthy that thou shouldest come under my roof: but*
*speak the word only, and my servant shall be healed.*

You do not hear Me when you pray; still, you must learn to listen
It's in this alone time with Me your Faith will grow and strengthen
Read My Word, sip a cup of coffee, and exit from noise pollution
Use a prayer book if you like, but make time for simple reflection

I Am with you at all times; that should fill your heart with passion
Every day I urge you, fear not, engage life boldly, without tension
Complete confidence in My presence, like that Roman Centurion
Only say the Word, he said, to heal my servant's dying condition

He knew all it takes is My healing touch; do you have such trust?
If you do, then why are you so driven? Fear is the sign of distrust
Exchange all worries for My peace and joy; in My love, stay robust
I need you to be healthy for service to My people whom I entrust

## February 29

## Imperfect Instruments Qualify

**John 15:4**
*Abide in me, and I in you. As the branch cannot bear fruit of itself, except it abide in the vine; no more can ye, except ye abide in me.*

Don't let the frenzy of work draw you away from time with Me
Even if you have a busy day, you'll gain more from our intimacy
Don't skip or cut our meetings short; I manage your profitability
My ways are higher than yours; yes, divine values are a mystery

You seek success in life; come to the Source for your excellence
Think of Moses, Joshua, and David's struggles and performance
Will you do a work for Me, then show Me courage, not impotence
Not by might or power, only My Spirit; in My Word is the evidence

Moses, David, Joshua, were imperfect instruments who qualified
They made mistakes like you; nonetheless, their work I sanctified
I expect excellence in My service, but I standby ready to rectify
Fret not about your weaknesses; My grace is sufficient to fortify

But do not be the incompetent person, powerless in service
Someone who tries very hard yet is a poor-quality apprentice
Worried over the future, knowing Me, but unbelieving like Judas
Rather be a risk taker willing to give it your all, in faithful practice

# March

## March 1

## God Is Love

**Proverbs 18:24**
*[A]nd there is a friend that sticketh closer than a brother.*

I left Heaven to die for My own, but My own did not appreciate
How do people scorn such Love? I long for them to reciprocate
My Divine Love created you My child, for I Am Love incarnate
It is the nature of Divine character to share Love, to disseminate

The Word became flesh; Divine becoming human in loving union
But what is Love if there is no exchange and no communication?
Do you sense that I, your Lord too, yearn for your reciprocation?
I call you friends; I died for you; I long for our tender interaction

I delight to see men seek Me not only for help but for conversation
There is so much to discuss, your interests, perhaps some situation
You are My little creator; I love to see your work coming to fruition
And what a joy it is when you invite Me to team up in collaboration

## March 2

## I Will Restore

**Hebrews 13:5**

*Let your conversation be without covetousness, and be content with such things as ye have: for he hath said, I will never leave thee, nor forsake thee.*

Nary a cry escapes My attention; *never* imagine I Am inattentive
Help Me! I hear people sob, but before I reply, they get inventive
They don't wait to know My will; they plunge into what's defective
Often serious trouble ensues, lives get ruined, and people captive

My Words are Spirit and Life; I approve of no haste in My Kingdom
Waiting for My response does not delay; it guarantees your freedom
Prosper in obedience to My Word; trust Me when you need wisdom
I delight in your initiatives, to see you triumph, not stuck in boredom

Commune with Me every day; gain all the insights you need to abide
In My Wisdom live, trust in My Grace, I Am your one reliable Guide
Look at My world; so many of My children try to make it alone in pride
I do not interfere with free will; I wait, hoping they bring Me alongside

Should you get into a difficult situation because you were disobedient
Fear not; there may be consequences for mistakes, not My punishment
Humbly explain what happened, trust Me, and never fear abandonment
I will restore what the locust has eaten and help you with management

I know what you would like Me to do and the quick fix you would prefer
But I've discerned why you got into trouble, so My solution might differ
I'll probably suggest some strict rules, which you must obey in the future
Yes, I will solve your problems if you trust in My Love, that is My offer

My child, you are not a robot; I created in you a magnificent sovereign will
In Love, I laid out the laws of life to comply with, for your good, not for ill
If you transgress My rules, difficulties ensue, you can end up going downhill
But let the world know that your Savior stands by you when you are in peril

# March 3

## No Other Ecstasy

**Ezekiel 37:14**

*And shall put my spirit in you, and ye shall live, and I shall place you in your own land: then shall ye know that I the Lord have spoken it, and performed it, saith the Lord.*

Do not follow those who try to communicate with their dead
Unclean spirits wait to lure the unsuspecting who go ahead
Heed the warnings in My Word and avoid the occult instead
Secrets of life and death are in the custody of the Godhead

Remember King Nebuchadnezzar troubled by his nightmare
But details of his ordeal forgotten, he was unable to declare
Chaldean sorcerers called to reveal the dream couldn't dare
God alone knew the secret, and Daniel was allowed to share

I have put My Spirit in you; there is nothing more you need
I Am the Lord your God; listen only to Me, to none else plead
As I was with My disciples, I Am with you; believe Me, heed
Our love story is the greatest; no other ecstasy can ever exceed

You have not the spirit of fear, but Power, Love, a sound mind
Abound in Joy, Peace, and Hope, My spiritual Power combined
These gifts I have bestowed, there is no greater love than mine
It is for you to use them in My Great Commission to humankind

## March 4

## Into My Likeness

**Philippians 1:6**

*Being confident of this very thing, that he which hath begun a good work in you will perform it until the day of Jesus Christ.*

You will change into My likeness if you constantly commune with Me
Do not let your sins overwhelm but get up when you fall; you are free
Your deep remorse confirms you are drawing closer to Me spiritually
I use your failures; nothing gets wasted in My Kingdom; you will see

Fear not, I will take all your weaknesses and I'll employ them usefully
Your struggles can hurt you only if you feel like a failure; that is a folly
Study My biblical characters; none were the perfect role models initially
My strength is made perfect in your weakness; you will change gradually

## March 5

## Be Humble

**Galatians 6:3**

*For if a man think himself to be something, when he is nothing, he deceiveth himself.*

Your relationship with Me is the medicine for every predicament
Sin or sorrow, it doesn't matter what the problem is; I Am present
Even before you were in the womb, I chose you as My instrument
I gauge obedience and trust; great success is not in My assessment

In the service of My Truth, remember that is not the world's appetite
People mostly prefer their worldly lusts; they all have their favorite
You must be patient when you debate salvation for lost souls to ignite
My Word is sharp enough to pierce hearts, but use it humbly and excite

Even among My followers, I see how they can fall prey to religious pride
Egoistic ambition and vain conceit are big hurdles; they spiritually collide
After the Fall, you don't have strength to do right unless in Me you abide
Self-control is among the fruit of My Spirit; it is a sign that I dwell inside

Whoever labors in My vineyard, starting early or late, gets paid equally
I do not attribute evil to My people, but My work calls for true humility
I was demeaned and shamed on Calvary; surrender pride, work with Me
It doesn't matter how people treat you; reacting with Love is a necessity

Discern the dangers in your work for Me; leading them is the sin of pride
Remember the proud Pharisees, so convinced that God was on their side
Spurning justice, mercy and faithfulness for greed, self-indulgence, inside
Messiah in flesh they denied, Sabbath keepers intent on spiritual suicide

Study your Servant King, and what do you see? Any pomp or majesty?
I humbled myself to the point of a shameful death, your Lord Almighty
In My service on earth, I was meek and merciful; never high and mighty
Greeting Me in Jerusalem royally, the same crowd would shout "Crucify!"

## March 6

## Fear Is Evil

**Proverbs 29:25**

*The fear of man bringeth a snare: but whoso putteth his trust in The LORD shall be safe.*

Start looking at your fears as evil; to control them better and overcome
I have not given you the spirit of fear; it is demonic, do not welcome
Scarcity, loneliness, unemployment, and disease bring you oppression
If you abide in Me, fear cannot hide in your heart, not in My Kingdom

Fear lurks everywhere, seeking to destroy individuals and nations
The great curse of the world it creates innumerable complications
Shatters Hope and Faith, a plague the Fall brought into My creation
It is one of My great enemies; do not ever try to use it for any reason

If you feel trapped in a cycle of fear, you are avoiding My Presence
Succumbing to the terrors that plague you due to your negligence
Perhaps some besetting sin got you under its control in My absence
Repent My child, trust My Love and mercy for a fear-free conscience

## March 7

## Labor of Love

**I Thessalonians 1:3**
*Remembering without ceasing your work of faith, and labour of love, and patience of hope in our Lord Jesus Christ, in the sight of God and our Father.*

Your life and work must be lived through Me; there is no other way
If you do not abide in Me, nothing will satisfy you, and you'll stray
When Love undergirds both Work and Life, every fear you can slay
Gently I led you into My Kingdom; your sins did not keep Me away

Hearts hardened by sin are like stony ground needing reclamation
Remember your journey to Me; it was hard to overcome depression
Your words, too, must build up; share grace in your communication
Never ashamed for rightly handling the Word of Truth in a situation

You must become as little children to enter the Kingdom of Heaven
See how they love and laugh in work and play, they are never driven
So, to work in My vineyard, be of good cheer for you are forgiven
No better Master can you find your merciful Lord's Love is proven

## March 8

## The Greatest Surprise

**Romans 6:23**
*For the wages of sin is death; but the gift of God is eternal life through Jesus Christ our Lord.*

You love surprises; I do too; it is not all about testing and training
Indeed, you must be My Cross bearers, but I care about your feelings
Hence a breakfast surprise for My disciples after a hard night of fishing
Disheartened and fearful by My Crucifixion, they needed much healing

I know your limits, and I will never stretch you beyond your endurance
I tested My disciples often, but I made sure they rested in My Presence
My miracles blessed all those I healed and gave My Apostles confidence
Surprises are in store for you, too; a life in Me is one of great significance

Your trust in your Savior, Love and Mercy is dear to My Father's heart
God so loved the world that He sent Me to die; for you, He set Me apart
Our tender rescue plan to save humanity We designed from the very start
Love's Greatest Surprise; Our eternal salvation in exchange for your heart

How much your Creator values His creation that God died in naked shame
For a sinful world that scorned the One who sought His own and became
Like a lamb led to the slaughter, I didn't open My mouth; I took the blame
Can you give up the world's lusts and pride to serve the lost in My name?

## March 9

## At My Command

**Psalm 89:9**

*Thou rulest the raging of the sea: when the waves thereof arise, thou stillest them.*

Happily, merrily welcome My new season; yours is the joy of Spring
Gone is the long winter; exult in the warmth that creation will bring
As swans and swallows start their yearly sojourn, I guide their wing
All this beauty and joy must tell you of My Love; let your heart sing

Giving you a taste of the paradise that Adam lost is for you My plan
Nature's comeliness and artistry Heaven's loving provision for man
But winter's not dead; there will come harsh seasons in your lifespan
Fear not; abide in Me to overcome your travails; I Am your Guardian

Paradise, I regained for you; oh! Fight the good fight for your prize
Even My apostles were alarmed that I would let their boat capsize
I manifested My creation in terrifying force; and they didn't realize
I command the wind and waves; learn My lessons, and I normalize

Let not your heart be troubled when earthly life's cold winds blow
More and more, you will realize the fullness of My Love and grow
It is through nature I exhibit beauty and ferocity for you to know
Look and learn from creation's incredible custom-designed show

When you feel vulnerable, remember in nature, I have holy intent
Seasons come and go, your struggle and tears build a commitment
Years of toil are like mountain heights, rest in all their wonderment
To the summit we both ascend; for you are My chosen instrument

Can life on earth be trouble-free? Not in My vineyard where I train
But My Love is stronger than every strain; all My workers I sustain
My Peace I guarantee all who believe in Me: they do not complain
Heavenly life beckons in this vale of tears, in My mysterious domain

## March 10

## No Greater Windfall

**Luke 12:6**

*Are not five sparrows sold for two farthings, and not one of them is forgotten before God?*

I delight in every single contribution; it doesn't matter how small
Every effort a sweet prelude to obtaining the rest of a higher Call
If a sparrow's life has value, how much more is your work overall
Eternal life I offered to all at Calvary; there is no greater windfall

You are My inheritance; do you see why you are My priceless prize
Pray for the Spirit of wisdom and revelation; understand and realize
I will not let you fall away, but your free will, I cannot neutralize
Even My mighty Power is helpless until you believe and vocalize

## March 11

## Fruit of Joy

**Psalm 135:6**
*Whatsoever the Lord pleased, that did he in heaven, and in earth, in the seas, and all deep places.*

Be still and know that I Am God; only then can our Spirits commune
Sight, hearing, touch, smell, and taste will keep material life in tune
But if you want to Spirit-converse with Me, these make you immune
Disconnect them all; rest your heart, enter My Silence, let's resume

People are similar at heart level, and that is where you must connect
But this happens only when you see the good in everyone, in respect
In humility, consider others better than yourself, for nobody is perfect
As you wish others would do to you, do to them; happiness will affect

Everyone's actions create ripples; few can understand My methodology
Laughter and affection make the world go round; My Love brings liberty

How you affect someone's life is hard to figure out; for I work in secrecy
Consider your interactions, bring My joy to all; you will live purposefully

## March 12

## I Will Astonish

**Matthew 6:26**

*Behold the fowls of the air: for they sow not, neither do they reap, nor gather into barns; yet your heavenly Father feedeth them. Are ye not much better than they?*

Wake up to the beauty of My exquisite creation; it's a new morning
In fiery Red Robins, Pink Cherry Blossoms, My Love is modeling
Salamanders appear, Golden Daffodils bloom; My glory is unfolding
Ten thousand expressions of My loving hopes for you they're bearing

Nature, I designed in style, awe and might; man needs more instruction
To be perfect as your heavenly Father, you only abide in My perfection
You are God's workmanship, created to do good in your Savior's union
Sin stains our divine artistry; My grace abounds for your transformation

But when you are inclined to disobey, think before you act and go astray
The Peace, laughter, joy, and fulfillment you cherish, sin quickly takes away
And Spring's grace and spiritual beauty is forgotten if you move faraway

Know this, My runaway child; I will be there waiting even when you betray

My Love for you nor man's scorn, nor a shameful death could diminish
Gently My heart whispers Truth, inspiration, and gladness till you finish
So, fear not, your Past, Present and Future challenges, we will vanquish
Seasons of life change; I will never leave you; I, your Lord, will astonish

Lilies of the field do not toil; they reflect My glory; every bird is in My care
Sing for Me with My creation, never be anxious, face all troubles with dare
Bask in My Love, laughing, serving, and giving; your loving kindness share
Then I know My beautiful world is in good hands; My work is your prayer

## March 13

## Do Not Conform

**James 4:6**
*But he giveth more grace. Wherefore he saith, God resisteth the proud,*
*but giveth grace unto the humble.*

From Heaven, I came, the Lord of the universe in plain, human form
My lowly birth in a stable announced My standard; humility, the norm
It's the cornerstone of My Kingdom; know I oppose pride in any form
Understand this clearly, never aspire to worldly ambition and conform

Live in the light as one caring, meek, and mild of a different parenthood
Beloved of God, covered by the grace He gives all in His neighborhood
Love and respect are My essential requirements; you have understood
You know that a simple life is enough; the love of money is a falsehood

What does it mean to live simply? Why do I oppose all those inflated?
Ignore trendy, minimalism; I look for minds transformed and contented
Free from worldly love, laser-focused on God's Kingdom, and devoted

Pursuing neither wealth nor ease nor glory nor an empire, all conceited

Fix your eyes on Me, and run the race I marked for you in perseverance
Reject the folly of chasing riches; do you trust Me? Present the evidence
Toil and achievement spring from envying one another, a form of violence
Seek the approval of God, not men; all these things have no significance

## March 14

## My Holy Spirit

**1 John 4:4**

*Ye are of God, little children, and have overcome them:*
*because greater is he that is in you, than he that is in the world.*

Many want a supernatural experience, and try out the spurious
Never trifle with the spirit world; it is very dark and dangerous
Unlike mediums, My Holy Spirit's work is humble; it's costless
For spiritual wisdom, ask your heavenly Father, He is generous

If you seek the Spirit-filled life, do not get involved in sorcery
Beloved, do not believe every spirit; test each one for treachery
If anyone does not acknowledge Me as Lord, it is evil trickery
My Word declares nine fruits of the Holy Spirit; it is no mystery

I said you would do greater works than I did; it is not without Me
To teach, remind, guide, and reveal, My Holy Spirit is your referee
If you give Him free rein, you will never need any other guarantee
No Holy Spirit; no new birth, no faith, no defeating sin, no victory

Unlocking mysteries of My Spirit Kingdom, the only key is Spiritual
Certain secrets will remain unknown to all who prefer the sensual

Paul's reference to the "third heaven" was real; it wasn't conceptual
Only when you're ready in Faith will I permit supernatural initiative

But remember, you are not to fear the evil one, that is not My intent
I do not want you wasting time on any evil in that futile environment
You are vulnerable only in besetting sin; then he demands a payment
You are in the world, not of the world, guarded by Me every moment

## March 15

## Free Will and Faithfulness

**Psalm 5:11**
*But let all those that put their trust in thee rejoice: let them ever shout for joy, because thou defendest them: let them also that love thy name be joyful in thee.*

Faith has no limits set by Me; it's your free will, your faithfulness
Look back at your life; I guide you step by step as you progress
I see if you obey My instructions gladly, watch you handle stress
You have received a trust; are you a worthy steward and witness?

When birds and beasts protect their young, they are not passive
On full alert, I watch your coming and going; I'm very protective
I Am your Lord, Maker of Heaven and earth, your Love, My motive
When you cry for help; I will rescue you whenever you fall captive

My hand hasn't shrunk, I will save, and My ear is always available
All your trials, troubles and your failures may seem insurmountable
They only serve My Will; when you join the family, I'm responsible
My Word says sin hides My face, My mercy and Love are intractable

I love to share your journey of life, so many experiences to discuss

Whatever comes your way can do no more than work to My purpose
But are you seeking to please man or God? Obey or be autonomous?
My provision, My Word, is enough even if you don't become famous

When you start the day, so many distractions claim more significance
You may wonder if the time we spend together makes any difference
But be confident, for every moment in Me becomes divine sustenance
For spiritual, intellectual, and material resources, you need My Presence

My child, as My Cross bearer, walk joyfully; do not give up but persevere
If you slip and fall into sin, get up and start again but do not be insincere
You lose the battle even before it has begun; My grace alone is your spear
So do not brood over your defeats; trust not in yourself, to Me draw near

## March 16

## Your Cross Is Self

**2 Corinthians 5:21**

*For he hath made him to be sin, who knew no sin; that we might be made the righteousness of God in him.*

My Word is interpreted as if I became sin, but evil to Me cannot cling
Latin and Hebrew, they both use the same word for sin and offering
I had to be sinless, a blemished lamb to My Father I could not bring
God never rejected Israel's sin offering because it was a holy thing

I ask you to take up your Cross daily, not to bear its sin like Mine
Your Cross is the weight of all that keeps you from My Life divine
You must crucify the self, or it is the idol, and you build its shrine
Do I not deserve your all? I've loved you since the dawn of time

Will you be My chosen instrument, or do you prefer your agenda?
You will do it your way; make money, fame, and power your saga
Lust of the flesh, and the eyes, the pride of life, make you go gaga
Forgetting My death and resurrection, you want Hollywood drama

I have a plan for your entire life; if you trust Me, have no anxiety
But what's your center of gravity? My Love and service, or a deity?
Are you enslaved to a cruel god, bound in chains by your naivety?
My yoke is easy, and My burden is light; fear not, I'll set you free

Anything that hinders you from service, I will remove and discard
I will move your feet to solid rock from sinking sand, I will guard
The harvest is plentiful; laborers few; I need you in My vineyard
Priceless is My salvation; no Master can offer you a greater reward

## March 17

## I Know What's Best

**Matthew 1:23**

*Behold, a virgin shall be with child, and shall bring forth a son, and*
*they shall call his name Emmanuel, which being interpreted is, God with us.*

There is a secret place in every heart where I reside, there we commune
Leave aside your worries; trust in Me alone, not in making your fortune
Share with Me your fears, hopes, and challenges; time in Me is opportune
I know what's best for you; let Me help you with your plans; I won't ruin

In the center of human hearts, I wait patiently, but few choose to meet
If only My people believed I did not create you to abandon on the street
Tossed and blown, your world out of control, you fearfully expect defeat
I did not design you to face your life in fear; My Presence, do not forfeit

You think you can make it in the dark all alone, your life a daily struggle
Unaided, you venture into the unknown where it's as risky as in the jungle

Would you let your child wander and fall into danger, leaving her single?
Nor have I, yet My unfailing Presence you ignore, in many perils mingle

Your God is with you; how can you forget and live in fear and doubt?
Stress and anxieties come when you have no time for Me; you dropout
Test My Truths against man's ingenuity, trust only in what checks out
Man has created wonders, but isn't your Maker's genius worth a shout?

I reside where the soul dwells, but only a few understand this reality
To discern and avoid spiritual dangers; you must live with Me in unity
My Truths are bandied about in error by many without My authority
Shun those who make you depend not on Me but on their personality

## March 18

## Live Your Adventure

**Joshua 1:9**
*Have not I commanded thee? Be strong and of a good courage; be not afraid, neither be thou dismayed: for the Lord thy God is with thee whithersoever thou goest.*

I tell you again; I Am your shield and great reward, your source of joy
You pursue satisfaction here and there in many things you won't enjoy
I'm the treasure store of wisdom; why ignore Me for what can destroy?
Your best interests I have at heart; trust Me with plans; I Am no killjoy

Heaven's host is amazed by people so reluctant to give Me their trust
For something terrible in their life, they will blame Me for being unjust
Many others wait until financial trouble comes when they may go bust
Know Me in life as your Savior now, not only in eternity; come discuss

When you face pressures that overwhelm and burdens you find too hard
It's because you do not habitually engage with Me in quiet; let Me guard
If you did, you would take tensions in your stride as My faithful steward

Why stress that time and tide wait not, eternity is yours in My
vineyard

You are not wrong to think about managing today and all your
tomorrows
But all who are mine; rest in Me; it's when life begins, not in the
shallows
I don't log years in My Kingdom; born twice, you surrender
your sorrows
Knowing Father, Son, and Holy Spirit is life eternal; new life
overshadows

So, forfeit your harried, driven life, your nagging fears about
the future
How foolish if the child of the Maker frets for provision and
expenditure
I Love you, and I will protect, sustain you, be fearless don't be
immature
Yes, your work matters; mine is your loving care; go live your
adventure!

## March 19

## One Source

**Hebrews 12:4**

*Ye have not yet resisted unto blood, striving against sin.*

Remember I said My Kingdom suffers violence and is taken by force
It's not for the sensual, ease-loving, who cannot muster the resource
Those who dare to assail its ramparts faithfully trust in their Life force
They will conquer it by their fervor and allegiance to only One Source

Consider so many martyrs down the ages from the time of My apostles
I warned I came not to send peace but a sword; they faced many perils
All but one died in the savagery unleashed on them, many kinds of evils
In every endeavor or the battle for My Kingdom, you must be invincible

In your never-ending fight against sin, I may not call you to shed blood
But learn from your forebears in Faith, how they all attained sainthood
Narrow is the way to life, unlike perdition's wide road; is it understood?
I Am your Source of Life; press in to reach and learn; avoid all falsehood

With the helmet of salvation, My Word as your sword, enter My Kingdom
You are no longer a slave; you are My heir; come and seize your freedom
Every longing of your heart, big or small, I already have on My agendum
Be bold and remember I stood by all who faced the lions in the Colosseum

## March 20

## Do Better Tomorrow

**Luke 12:29**
*And seek not ye what ye shall eat, or what ye shall drink, neither be ye*
*of doubtful mind.*

Never let troubles turn into fears; they are only a fleeting examination
Instead, ask yourself, where did I go wrong, and what is the explanation?
In all likelihood, the answer lies within you, quite likely in your motivation
Your lack of trust or disobedience; regardless, in Me there's no condemnation

Do you trust Me, the Maker of heaven and earth, you see I need to know
No man is fit for My Kingdom who looks back with his hand on the plow
But I Am the God of Love and mercy, all who cry for help; I will not forego
Courage, My child, every morning is a fresh new day, do better tomorrow

Many live their lives afraid, but life shouldn't frighten you at all; I Am here
Things will go wrong; they sometimes do; life is quite curvy; it's not linear

In sunrise and sunset, you are not alone; I will never be gone; so, persevere
I designed you to succeed, not only survive; all is well, be of good cheer

## March 21

## Be Faithful

**Malachi 3:10**

*Bring ye all the tithes into the storehouse, that there may be meat in mine*
*house, and prove me now herewith, saith the Lord of hosts, if I will not*
*open you the windows of heaven, and pour you out a blessing, that there*
*shall not be room enough to receive it.*

When you engage in unwise pursuits that harm and bring you no benefit
So much of life is compromised and your learning delayed for less profit
Yes, it is true; I can use every situation for good, but why do what's unfit?
Whether it's trivial or terrific, whatever you do for Me is all to your credit

Don't you appreciate someone who carries out your wishes faithfully?
In the workplace, the person who excels gets awarded professionally
But I don't evaluate as the world does; I consider all things eternally
So you may not succeed at all you do, just give Me your heart totally

Do not engage in anything remotely contradicting My will and authority
You needn't depend on anyone else, for I Am your provider and security
I ensure you obtain what you need in many ways from the community
It could be friends, family or perhaps My angels given the responsibility

## March 22

## Your Escort

**Exodus 33:14**
*And he said, My presence shall go with thee, and I will give thee rest.*

Whenever you are in doubt, anticipate the best, declare "All is well"
It's to show you trust Me implicitly; it's not a mantra or magic spell
Your life is a journey I have already planned; follow Me, and dwell
You are not alone; I Am always with you; every trouble I will dispel

When things get tough, I watch to see if you will panic or proceed?
Your reaction indicates trust; it tells Me how much help you'll need
But there are times when you must fast and pray, and you'll be freed
There is never a situation for despair; for My Presence is guaranteed

You must work your work; I mine; the path is rough; in a life so short
Souls toiling with Me in My blessed work to save, know and report
Long hard days wane in a rare peace, bringing joy, and much comfort

So strive to seek, to find, and not to yield; for I Am always your escort

## March 23

## Life's Essence

**Matthew 6:8**

*Be not ye therefore like unto them: for your Father knoweth what things ye have need of, before ye ask him.*

When it is about meeting your needs, I always prepare the best
Nonetheless, I love to interact with you to see what you suggest
I want to know, are you managing life and work, are you stressed?
Are your dreams shattered, My child? Is it your aim to be famous?

I love to see you reach for the stars, wisely employ all your talents
But those who aim for My Kingdom must meet some requirements
The world covets fame and glory; I need service and commitment
Your faithfulness merits, "Well done, My good and faithful servant"

Yes, I know you need money and often you wonder if I will deliver
Men fear poverty, scorn the poor; I want you free, don't love silver
I can multiply loaves and fishes; you have no worries whatsoever
Money can be a hair shirt; use it in My wisdom, don't be a doubter

If you're worth it, you'll make it, is how the world thinks and expounds

You want Me to get specific? Let's say you need ten thousand pounds
You'd like to win a lottery or get a gift from a friend, someone known
Giving you the money is not the issue, are your motives clearly shown?

I own the cattle on a thousand hills; I can pick a rose or extract gold
I want you to understand that no need gets neglected in My household
Why someone is rich, while another becomes poor is a mystery to unfold
It does seem unfair, but one day, you will learn My reasons to withhold

But before you succumb to life's daily lacerations on your spirit
Observe how many in far worse circumstances have found merit
Entrepreneurs and others who employed talents for great profit
I provide some skill to all; overcome as they do, to your credit

Among My great creators you can find the poorest of the poor
Your ordinary neighbors: and you thought they were a bore
Artists, writers, healers, and others, despite lack, deliver more
In My Kingdom riches don't make a difference, you can score

Providing for you means more than helping you gain affluence
Haven't I performed a miracle for you in a difficult circumstance?
A spiritual aspect is in every situation you face; it is life's essence
I call you to be holy, active, joy-filled, not merely enjoy existence

## March 24

## Do Not Despair

**Isaiah 41:10**

*Fear thou not; for I Am with thee: be not dismayed; for I Am thy God.*

I Am your complete protection; reject all your anxiety and fear
Observe My creation, My great beasts and the cubs they rear
Their lives are brief, their dangers many, yet calm they appear
I note the sparrow's fall; I Am more ferocious than Mother bear

Despite the evidence, man is unconvinced of the power of prayer
Your earnest plea can transform any situation needing My care
When you falter on the pilgrim trail, as you will, cry out and share
Battle-scarred and weary, waiting for your miracle, do not despair

Consider the heartfelt prayers of My servants portrayed in the Bible
Some were weak, woeful sinners, a faith in some cases questionable
Trembling souls who clung to Me, their feeble hearts were culpable
These suppliants I could have castaway, I did not make them liable

Abraham, My man of faith, was deceitful, calling wife Sarah his sister
He lied twice to Pharaoh and Abimelech, fearing for his life, the matter

But he left his home in Ur at My command, which showed Me character
His titanic test was My demand to sacrifice Isaac; he trusted his Master

David, I called a man after My own heart, an adulterer and murderer
Nonetheless pardoned, he models My great mercy as My torchbearer
Power and Love belong to Me; if sin overcomes, I Am your Savior
I long for faithfulness, but I won't abandon you even as a wanderer

Jonah got swallowed by a great whale, a lesson for his disobedience
His poignant petition to the Father is a beautiful prayer of repentance
From the realm of the dead, he cried for help; he got a second chance
"Salvation comes from the Lord," he said, grateful in My forbearance

So, when you get hurled into the depths, into the currents of the deep
The engulfing waters may threaten, or your mountain may look steep
Remember, He who watches over you does neither slumber nor sleep
Be steadfast in prayer; know you are protected; My promise I will keep

## March 25

## Your Tomorrows

**Isaiah 51:1**

*Hearken to me, ye that follow after righteousness, ye that seek the Lord: look unto the rock whence ye are hewn, and to the hole of the pit whence ye are digged.*

Establish your faith in Me, nothing else; build a genuine relationship
Live your life for Me, and watch everything fall into place in My grip
Practice My constant Presence, don't let distractions make you trip
As much as you need Me, I also wait for your loving companionship

My Word has all the wisdom you need to gain a deeper foundation
I know you'd like to know the future; you don't need that revelation
Let alone what's hidden, remember Faith is your priceless possession
Citizenship in My Kingdom offers you sanctuary; seek no other region

Find a quiet place to be in My Presence; don't hide in the shadows
Do not forget Me in the battle of life, then worry about tomorrows
Weeds of self-doubt will grow without Me; you live in the shallows
But time with the God of your salvation will overcome all sorrows

## March 26

## Lead My People

**1 Peter 4:10**

*As every man hath received the gift, even so minister the same one to another, as good stewards of the manifold grace of God.*

Dwell on the wonders of life; you received at least one experience
Blessed with talents and spiritual gifts, you must make a difference
Your heavenly Father desires you to impart His love and influence
Be a faithful witness to His goodness, and share your inheritance

Measure success not only by your gain but at least one left behind
Each of My children are sacred, endowed with gifts but often blind
Some make an early start in My Kingdom; some need you to be kind
Every one of them is a unique child of God, a masterpiece in My mind

Life's greatest wonder is the salvation of one with your helping hand
Remember, My Great Commission is no suggestion, but My command
Keep that in mind and persist in My service, inspire all and withstand
I empowered you to guide and heal, lead people to My promised land

## March 27

## Follow Your Guide

**Psalm 22:19**
*But be not thou far from me, O Lord: O my strength, haste thee to help me.*

Your doubts and fears are baseless; cast them all away
When anxieties seem too much to handle, there is a way
Do whatever you can do, leave the rest to Me, and pray
After that, if you continue worrying, you keep Me at bay

Your challenges may be like having to ford a mighty river
Against that magnificent terrain, will you fear and shiver?
If you are aware of My Presence, you must know I deliver
I planned your journey; every obstacle you will crossover

Remember My people Israel cornered before the Red Sea
The hounding Egyptian army in pursuit, confident of victory
I tore the deep apart and My people walked on dry land free
Are you at the Red Sea? Doubting or trusting in My reality?

Life is a series of battles; I've provided the weapons you need
Above all, I Am your Guide; with My help, you will succeed
But don't succumb to worldly desires; never give in to greed
When it comes to buying and selling, be wise, do not exceed

When the day is over, will you be grateful or fear the morrow?
Do you see how foolish it is to dwell on doubts to add sorrow?
Sometimes, if the skies are cloudy, why does your life torpedo?
What's painful today will be memories healing you tomorrow

## March 28

## For No Merit

**Psalm 32:3–4**

*When I kept silence, my bones waxed old through my roaring all the day long. For day and night thy hand was heavy upon me: my moisture is turned into the drought of summer. Selah.*

There is Power, wonder-working Power in My Holy Spirit
Godly Power, Love, and a Sound Mind; yours for no merit
Your life renews, for you will enter into My heavenly orbit
You will sing a new song when My sweet Spirit you inherit

Time invested in My Word is a force that many do not realize
Its impact greater than any discipline man tries to exercise
Any human undertaking, no matter how clever the enterprise
If you grasp this reality, your everyday routine will surprise

When skies are dark and storms appear, do you pray in fear?
Secretly trying to conceal the guilt in your heart is insincere
What your tormented conscience feels, I know, and I Am near
Ask for help to start life anew, all you need is My Spirit's spear

Amidst your distress, when troubles and temptations burden
Tossed either with despair or doubt, sometimes they're sudden
When earthly passions overcome My Truth, fear not; I embolden
Your sins confessed, My Sweet Spirit will comfort and gladden

## March 29

## The Amazing Folly

**2 Chronicles 30:9**
*For the Lord your Grace is gracious and merciful, and will not*
*Turn away his face from you, if ye return unto him.*

My grace is free, that is the Truth, and it does not demand obedience
But without a repentant heart, it cannot flow, then it meets resistance
Grace is not a license to sin; it is My Love for you and the evidence
Only your free will to choose or reject Me can cancel your inheritance

For if grace is conditional, how can it be the Good News for mankind?
The incredible folly of God's Love for sinners, that mystery so sublime
My mercies are new every morning; I don't want to leave anyone behind
Grace is limitless; you are free; but accept My Love, make up your mind

## March 30

## Whatever Comes

**Psalm 34:17**
*The righteous cry, and the Lord heareth, and delivereth them out of all their troubles.*

You are in the world, not of the world; you must stay apart
Free, confident of My Love, for you've given Me your heart
Go forth boldly; live and serve, save, and perform your part
Walk with Me, don't run on; from My Presence, don't depart

Your struggles are brief; can you bear with them for My sake?
Our quiet times together become the balm you need to take
Let nothing out there daunt, no hardship, stress, or mistakes
I Am your God; fear not, whatever comes, I will never forsake

In this vale of tears, sometimes you will fall if you do not abide
My apostles had passions like you, vulnerable even by My side
You are not sinless; that only happens when in Me you've died
Nothing can sabotage or harm, courage and joy! I Am your Guide

## March 31

## Your Testimonial

**John 4:39**

*And many of the Samaritans of that city believed on him for the saying of the woman, which testified, He told me all that ever I did.*

Some think an attitude of quiet resignation in life is spiritual
That passive stance is not to be adopted; it is not beneficial
Come what may, joyful, anticipating hearts are My testimonial
Thankful for blessings, unafraid, and confident of My potential

I Am watching over you; what can trouble you in My Presence?
Seeing you carefree, loving and laughing affirms your resilience
Worship in grace and holiness; let earth fear in God's residence
You are mine, rest in My Love, be thankful for your deliverance

# April

## April 1

## Welcome Trials

**2 Corinthians 12:9**

*And he said unto me, My grace is sufficient for thee: for my strength is made perfect in weakness. Most gladly therefore will I rather glory in my infirmities, that the power of Christ may rest upon me.*

My child, spiritual lessons take time to learn, but I Am patient
You are in the world, the domain after the Fall of the Serpent
But you must learn to overcome even in his evil environment
My Word is your lamp and Light; the Power needed to repent

As you master My teachings, you will learn to overcome
To stand in Faith in every situation when it is worrisome
All hope seems lost, and you have no idea of the outcome
Your weakness is My strength; let your trials be welcome

Down the ages, can you see from the deaths of My martyrs
Their courage came from My real Presence, not their powers
Timid, faithless apostles became leaders, healers, conquerors
No command, wisdom or counsel stands against My followers

## April 2

## Power to Change

**Colossians 3:5**
*Mortify therefore your members which are upon the earth; fornication, uncleanness, inordinate affection, evil concupiscence, and covetousness, which is idolatry.*

My Presence is certain; I Am with you, have no doubt, this is crucial
At times you will feel all alone; know it's all for testing your potential
When you fall into sin, fear not; always start anew, even if it is serial
I Am here to bless and help you, not condemn; My Love is perennial

Everything is by My Word, from lowest depths to the highest heights
Without discipline and study, you cannot understand or gain insights
My dauntless miracle-workers, in their obedience, are heavyweights
But know it's not what you can do; it's who you are—My great delight

Working great miracles comes from My Holy Spirit's power to change
Reborn in My Word, you transform, new robes of Faith you exchange

As I reconstruct your character, you mature and meet every challenge
Growing into My likeness, wearing the robe of righteousness, I arrange

# April 3

## Great Servanthood

**Philippians 2:7**
*But made himself of no reputation, and took upon him the form of a servant,*
*and was made in the likeness of men.*

The Lord of heaven and earth, Creator of the universe, I Am your servant
At the beck and call of all My children, on full alert, I Am never dormant
Whatever the situation, tell Me what is happening; My Love is constant
I died for you, My child, shedding My blood for an everlasting covenant

Learn from Me about great servanthood, and live your life with purpose
My salvation comes to the humble, but many choose to be autonomous
Let humility and obedience mark your service; that is a duty continuous
Freely you have received, freely share, My Love understood, is infectious

## April 4

## Kingdom Values

**Mark 4:11**
*And he said unto them, Unto you it is given to know the mystery of the kingdom*
*of God: but unto them that are without, all these things are done in parables.*

I Am in the business of transforming lives, but it's not always instant
Vain men and women, aloof and disdainful, are like taming an elephant
The proud I will oppose, the humble I seek to bring into My covenant
In human affairs, mistakes are costly; My Kingdom values are different

I chose humble fishermen as My apostles to receive My Holy Spirit
Often coarse, faithless, and disobedient, without theological merit
But through their weaknesses, I taught them their mission to inherit
It's your failings I use to equip you for service, but only if you submit

Empowering impetuous Peter would have been folly for his weakness
If he was proud and arrogant not broken, pliant for spiritual progress

Betraying Me is a great sin; like Peter, you too will test My forgiveness
Only then are you ready to speak of your Savior as My faithful witness

Again and again, My Word makes it clear your sins I do not number
But spiritual life is more subtle than the flesh; you must remember
Any wrong even by a hair's breadth is known no matter how clever
If you fault, I correct, you return; My Love is constant whatsoever

Go to the field and see, one stalk bends low, another tall and haughty
Gather both and examine; the one bent low has grain, the other empty
That is how it is with people; proud, rich, and clever claim sovereignty
Despite their grand achievements, in My Kingdom, they gain no entry

## April 5

## Of No Consequence

**Micah 7:8**

*Rejoice not against me, O mine enemy: when I fall, I shall arise; when I sit in darkness, the Lord shall be a light unto me.*

Human relationships can become idol worship if you get deceived
When you depend on someone, believe they alone meet your need
That allegiance belongs to Me, and My Love for you is guaranteed
Every human heart is a sealed book, and its pages only I can read

Whenever you make time for Me, it's an investment in My Presence
If there's an experience on earth more rewarding, show Me evidence
Share the good and bad with Me daily; I Am waiting to give guidance
I love to see you engaging in life; your failures are of no consequence

# April 6

## Complete Trust My Demand

**John 11:25–26**
*Jesus said unto her, I Am the Resurrection, and the life: he that believeth in me, though he were dead, yet shall he live: And whosoever liveth and believeth in me shall never die. Believest thou this?*

Shun all earthly treasures, and hold fast only to My saving hand
I bless you in My tender touch; it's Easter, new life, My command
Death and sin I trampled; there is nothing to fear, only understand
Let go of anxiety for the future; your complete trust is My demand

Often you cry out for My blessing, but something has you in its grip
Something or someone keeps you in bondage or some big ego trip
I call out to you, and you don't listen; life is best under My kingship
Break free from all attachments this Easter; I Am worthy of worship

## April 7

## The Mystery

**John 3:15**

*That whosoever believeth in him should not perish but have eternal life.*

Sin is death, trampled in My Resurrection; its potential I've crucified
It is finished, not to be feared; defeated, for its power I have destroyed
Mankind's sins I have forgiven; eternal life is free for all who will abide
But sin clings, tries the flesh; knows you were mysteriously sanctified

Loathe the world; your autonomy-demanding Self is acutely stubborn
Like a grain of wheat dies to yield fruit, carnal appetites you must scorn
Die to lusts; of the eyes, flesh, pride of life, and in Me, you will be reborn
Redeemed by your Savior, eternal life, My prize will crown your sojourn

## April 8

## Marks of the Kingdom

**Matthew 5:20**

*For I say unto you, That except your righteousness shall exceed the righteousness of the scribes and Pharisees, ye shall in no case enter into the kingdom of heaven.*

Many call Me Lord, Lord to enter My Kingdom, with only lip service
One foot kept in the world; they try to live on the edge of a precipice
When they try to entice you, do not yield but flee from their midst
Stand apart even if they mock you as a fool for being My apprentice

It is your heart I desire; there is no other gift I want you to bring
But no gift do I refuse, no matter how humble the smallest offering
A bad habit overcome, a relationship restored, a new skill in training
Some little change to show you are trying; My love is transforming

It is Easter; has My Resurrection life made any noticeable difference?
I Am thrilled you do not love your old fond ways, and there is evidence

Where there was chaff, I can see a grain of wheat for your persistence
Strive only for Me, nothing else; in My vineyard, receive all guidance

# April 9

## What's the Worry?

**Exodus 9:16**

*And in very deed for this cause have I raised thee up, for to shew in thee my power; and that my name may be declared throughout all the earth.*

Dismiss whatever hinders your risen life; My death is your victory
Easter's great lesson is My Love is *whole*—it is tangible, not theory
Grasp that, and you will lose all your fears, in whatever category
You don't have to fear sin and death, so tell Me, *what's the worry*?

Where you went wrong, change course, it's a chance to re-imagine
You have a clean slate; rewrite your life story; a joyful chapter begin
Break free of doubt and dread, take risks; the territory is new, virgin
Nothing can harm you now; your future is in My hands to determine

Find My purpose for your life; a true witness can transform humanity
I have equipped and armed you, conquer all phantoms in My security
In My holiness, joy, peace, and love, live and work to your total capacity
Will you choose this day your vain ambitions or serve under My authority?

Each day interpret the spirit of the tomb and the Spirit of My Resurrection
One makes you driven; the other revitalizes you for My Great Commission
In Me, live, move, have your being; discern the *Be* in Me, *Do* in Me tension
Your risen life proclaiming, "I live, yet not I, but Christ liveth in Me" union

## April 10

## I Am Love

**1 John 4:8**
*He that loveth not knoweth not God; for God is love.*

I Am Love, so must you be, do not run after it; Love is Me in you
*Be* in Me, do not allow phony love to get your feelings confused
It is vital to grasp *My* Love; you cannot obey Me when bemused
When Love and Obedience meet, the key to My Kingdom is fused

Your obedience, I know, is you walking on unfinished stone stairs
You climb up; you fall down; I wait for you to bounce back upstairs
As long as you do not stay down and give up, you will not despair
For I will never leave you nor forsake you, through all your affairs

Home is where the heart is; you often hear it said among friends
So it is with Me; the humblest sinful heart is My home that mends
But I can only dwell in lowly hearts; the proud will meet their ends
Pride as sentinel, expels the meek Christ; death it cannot transcend

## April 11

## Stand Your Ground

**Matthew 17:20**

*And Jesus said unto them, Because of your unbelief: for verily I say unto you, If ye have faith as a grain of mustard seed, ye shall say unto*
*this mountain, Remove hence to yonder place; and it shall remove; and nothing shall be impossible unto you.*

Called to be a peculiar people, I've set you apart for My purpose
But look around; so many go their way, and you too can choose
To be lured by your ambitions or My Love to spread the Good News
Your choices must differ, and motives not what the world has fused

Pray My Love reaches all who cross your path, for they are in need
If anyone rejects you, do not take offence, your job is only to seed
Discipline and difference mark My work, My Spirit of Love to succeed
Never yield; you can move mountains in Faith if you and I are agreed

## April 12

## Have No Pride

**Philippians 2:8**

*And being found in fashion as a man, he humbled himself, and became*
*obedient unto death, even the death of the cross.*

Your Guide is the Maker of heaven and earth; such power if you trust
Failures are only something brief; without Faith, life itself will crush
Can I help someone who will not believe? I do and often get rebuffed
Still, I will respond even before you ask; call Me; life can get engulfed

Your need is My chance to help you; be your support, come alongside
Whatever the situation, no matter your sins, to save, I have no pride
Faith, when given expression, is the opportunity for My power to reside
It is the key that opens the vault of My resources, to take what is inside

You may see your failures; I see humble servants striving for progression
Just as a mother ignores her child's mistakes, I aid in your transformation

Do not be discouraged when you fail; with Me never lose communication
My Love sees your feeble allegiance and awards you My divine perfection

## April 13

## Keep Life Simple

**Isaiah 42:3**
*A bruised reed shall he not break, and the smoking flax*
*shall he not quench: he shall bring forth judgment unto truth.*

I designed you to love and laugh, not to brood and despair
Make a difference in your world by making it much happier
In nature and life, I have created variety, desert, and glacier
It's hot or cold, rain or drought, wind, or calm in My frontier

One day in the wilderness, next your mountaintop experience
Regard both as faithful duty, cheerfully executed in balance
In hardship, prove to be gentle; many live a painful existence
See hearts as I do, walk in their shoes, share My abundance

Let Me be your go-between when you meet any hurting people
A bruised reed I will not break, nor let the faint of heart topple
In prayer and My Presence is your rest; keep your life simple
Work has its rewards; persist in all you do as My true disciple

## April 14

### From Weakness

**Acts 10:34–35**

*Then Peter opened his mouth, and said, Of a truth I perceive that God is no respecter of persons: But in every nation he that feareth him, and worketh righteousness, is accepted with him.*

I Am your faithful Guide; My Light overcomes the darkness
All you have to do is keep Me in sight when you face distress
I turn your failings into blessings, draw strength from weakness
In My vineyard, I will never disqualify you for lack of progress

You balance life's failures and victory, if you consider both profit
In My Kingdom, I value all efforts; success or defeat, you benefit
See tension in every situation as something abnormal; deal with it
Harmony centers in Me; I bring poise, and every stress you forfeit

I gave you a vision; if faithfully executed, it will clear every hurdle
When you glimpse My purpose for you, sighting it is like a candle
Spiritual light is yours, power to undertake My work, to enkindle
Lose no time seeking more direction; your mission is ready, visible

I left many things unsaid to My disciples that they couldn't bear
But to all who follow Me faithfully, I communicate, and I declare

I know sometimes it is hard to understand; My Will seems unclear
Listen carefully for My voice; only when you keep still do I share

I gave Simon Peter a vision for the Gentiles he did not understand
Until My Spirit pointed to three men Cornelius sent at My command
Then the Apostle saw I favor no man, but I accept all into My hand
From every nation, anyone humble and teachable fits into My plan

## April 15

## The Difference

**Revelation 3:8**
*I know thy works: behold, I have set before thee an open door, and no man can shut it: for thou hast a little strength, and hast kept my word, and hast not denied my name.*

Keep calm; it is a sign you *know* Me; success hides in obedience
Retreat into silence in any distress; you only need My assurance
Remember, I Am with you always, live peacefully in My Presence
Not even a moment spent with Me is fruitless; that's the difference

If you ever get messages that you are inadequate, it is not My voice
I created you with wisdom and strength in My very image for office
Remember, My Spirit flows in humble hearts even if you are a novice
That's how My work gets accomplished by all who are in My service

Claim My Power every day, every hour, for every task; it is essential
Employ your God-given talents, and you'll produce work exceptional
Abide in Me and be complete, or you cannot reach your full potential
Why disregard My Love, not claim My help, to invite failure and trial?

## April 16

## What Truly Matters

**Romans 13:8**

*Owe no man any thing, but to love one another: for he that loveth another hath fulfilled the law.*

When you are certain of My Love, no matter your experience
You know the secret of loving others is My abiding Presence
I Am the source of life; in My Love, you can make a difference
Love all on your path; remember, I loved all at every instance

I loved the lepers and the blind, scorned as the friend of sinners
Your heavenly Father's unchanging love has unmerited favors
My child, you must imitate His Love, for it is what truly matters
In Me is no lack of forgiveness, and so it must be in My followers

Do everything in Love as your Father watches you from heaven
No fault-finding, no bitterness, but a genuine humility beholden
With a passion for God and man, obedience for being forgiven
Bear no ill to your neighbor, love fulfills the law; it is written

## April 17

## What Is Joy?

**James 1:2–3**
*My brethren, count it all joy when ye fall into divers temptations;*
*Knowing this, that the trying of your faith worketh patience.*

What is a parent's joy? A loving, obedient, eager son or daughter
Or a difficult teen, willful and resigned in attitude and character?
I long for hearts yearning to do My Will, thirsty for My living water
Resignation, more than unbelief, deters My Love; won't let Me enter

When you force the Self to resign its hold on you, it is My delight
When you gladly choose My Will as a disciple, you claim your right
You start your apprenticeship in wonder and joy as our hearts unite
But life is a college of learning, and My lessons don't always excite

You wrestle with doubts and challenges until you value My training
So much to learn, so much I must teach you, be sure you're gaining
I Am with you in your struggles; I feel your pain when you're failing
I give strength to confront your fears; My joy comes in the morning

Unseen you forget My Presence, of My Joy there seems no evidence
Count your blessings, see My interventions and My steady guidance
Humble hearts hear My still, small voice; they know My persistence
Your thankfulness, rejoicing, awe, trust, and praise follow in sequence

The joy of the Lord is your strength, a gift that's far more than revelry
It is the fruit of My Spirit, obtained in obedience to My Will in humility
In your journey of discipline, defeat, and perhaps despair occasionally
Live out your Faith, overcome doubt and fear, bouncing back regularly

It is the joy no man can take from you, rest in My Love with confidence
Know all your burdens are mine; you are My witness; make a difference
In whatever state you are, learn to be content, trust even in turbulence
Laugh with Me at all your fears; every gift of mine is your inheritance

## April 18

## To All in Need

**Romans 8:32**

*He that spared not his own Son, but delivered him up for us all, how shall he not with him also freely give us all things?*

Share My Love with all who cross your path; help those you can
God is Love; to whomever you lend a helping hand, it's in My plan
Situations you can't handle, bring them to Me; I Am their Guardian
To all in need, a kind word of cheer, for the weakest are My children

You cannot help them all, but you can share My Love; it is sufficient
Comforting the least of mine, you comfort Me; you are My instrument
I send them trusting you; if you do not care, imagine My predicament
You said you would carry My Cross; in truth, wasn't that a commitment?

You promised Me a home in your heart; at your word, I came to reside
I observe your coming and going, know your actions from the inside
Teach fellow sinner-travelers their Savior longs for them to confide
My Love exceeds all they fear; on their journey home, I Am their Guide

If all shared My Love, there would be no hell on earth for sinfulness
God's image seen in every human face; there would be no bitterness
None without a friend; sorrow's cup drained of its dregs, would bless
Men would know their heavenly Father, keenly share His goodness

## April 19

## There Is a Way

**Acts 17:25**

*Neither is worshipped with men's hands, as though he needed any thing, seeing he giveth to all life, and breath, and all things.*

In the broken world you live, people desperately cry in urgent need
Ignored by many with plenty, greedy for more and more to succeed
But you are My workmanship; it is My Calling and purpose you heed
Generosity to the poor lends to the Lord, and I will repay every deed

Bless every troubled heart; that's what I need you for as My witness
Many ignore their Maker to live free, and they get driven to distress
Unaware there is Strength, Rest, Joy, Calm and Tenacity, I possess
Tell them their Lord is like none on earth; I Am their true happiness

Safe in the bosom of My Love, for all the wonder of divine intimacy
They can leave it all to Me and find all they missed in life's love story
Yes, it's incredible, nigh inconceivable, how you obtain eternal legacy
The joy of discovering there is a way not based on man's meritocracy

## April 20

## My Treasure

**2 Timothy 1:10**

*But is now made manifest by the appearing of our Saviour Jesus Christ,*
*who hath abolished death, and hath brought life and immortality to light*
*through the gospel.*

The greatest and the worst event in history ever, Calvary modeled
On an unhewn Cross, I hung alone, rejected, mutilated and mangled
Reopening Paradise to save My fallen creation, on a tree, I dangled
Giving you the Good News, death and sin are both forever trampled

Are your troubles unbearable, My child? Haven't I made a difference?
I love to see you meet all your challenges with complete confidence
Your grit, patience, and humility thrill Me; they tell of your obedience
Such is the joy you bring to My heart, of your loving trust, the evidence

I remember the agony of nails piercing My hands and feet at Calvary
But when wounded by My friends, it's more agonizing, not secondary

Every doubt and fear grieves Me, all confusion sent by the Adversary
I treasure your gratitude when you tell Me I Am your safe sanctuary

# April 21

## The Good News

**Song of Solomon 2:4**

*He brought me to the banqueting house, and his banner over me was love.*

I have redeemed you; sin and death are powerless in My Presence
Sin will rear its ugly head only if you disobey; keep Me at a distance
Practice abiding in Me constantly, as you keep breathing in cadence
All who believe in My name receive My salvation as their deliverance

Many don't grasp the *Good News*; the Lord's favor to which I pointed
Liberty for captives, prisoners, the oppressed and all the brokenhearted
In Jerusalem's synagogue, what did the scripture mean that I completed?
What is special if God rewards only the good and punishes the perverted?

For all those who understand God's grace, the gates of Paradise fly open
All who trust in Me, their sins are forgiven; it's My miracle gift of salvation
You cannot earn it with a do-it-yourself spirituality; it will cause frustration

Grace is God's fantastic folly; though no one is worthy, yet He chooses union

The scandal of My gospel's *Good News* is, I Am not passive in My loving
I scatter your sins as far as the East from the West to make you beguiling
In My furious Love you will know your God, understand My divine yearning
Forget all squalid choices and failures; hasten to your Lover; I Am waiting

Once you drink of My living water, earthly thirst quenchers cannot prevail
If you practice My Presence, sinful interests fade; you will exit evil's trail
But salvation though free, cannot be forced; you have a free will to avail
Freedom forever, but it is your resolve; do you want to escape from jail?

## April 22

## Reliable Provision

**James 1:8**
*A double minded man is unstable in all his ways.*

Laugh at your troubles; a tiny black dot on a white paper can entice
In life's vast canvas, see the rainbow, not the speck in your service
Trust me always, even if you fail, till it's over, you are My apprentice
Follow Me obediently, worry not for supply, My yoke is easy, rejoice

Workers in My vineyard are baffled by My system of management
The first may be last, and vice versa; My unique divine assessment
But everyone's share is enough, there's no need for any resentment
That's how it is in My employ; I know your needs as My instrument

Seeking My Kingdom and also seeking affluence is double minded
Indicates you want to keep one foot in the world; you are undecided
Anxious and distrusting of My supply; maybe you often feel stranded
But fear not, My child, recount your blessings; I have always provided

My disciple's supply is custom delivered according to your situation
But you may see those you consider undeserving in a better condition
Men engage in labor differently; most reliable of all is My provision
Great wealth is more often a risk, not an asset, nor My commendation

## April 23

## Follow Me

**Psalm 4:3**
*But know that the Lord hath set apart him that is godly for himself.*

Abide in Me, and I will transform your doubts into confidence
Be at peace in My rest; no need to constantly ask for guidance
I Am the Vine; you are My branches; only realize My Presence
It is your heart's surrender I care about, not your performance

Fresh fruit hangs low on the tree, but how was it manufactured?
Can the branches take credit? No, the abiding in the vine mattered
Silently we work in harmony; My Life is the conduit, favored
Our union is indispensable; and your need for My Spirit is sacred

Be alert to My Spirit's teaching in sharing your Faith to witness
People are not impressed with words; they can sense and assess
When we commune, I rarely use words; follow Me in the process
You have a unique role in the harvest; it will lead you to success

Are you called to be a sower, reaper, or spotter, to gather or water?
At home or in business or wander as an itinerant, a humble preacher?
I have set you apart; wherever the harvest is, be My faithful worker
We'll face the hardships in your journey; I'll never forsake you, ever

## April 24

## Only Progress

**John 21:11**
*Simon Peter went up, and drew the net to land full of great fishes, a hundred and fifty and three: and for all there were so many, yet was not the net broken.*

I Am the Resurrection and the Life; death is a brief transit, powerless
Born of My Spirit, eternal life yours, you cannot perish, only progress
Confront danger, adversity, and sorrow; all these should not distress
Down the ages, I have kept My people; I lose none, in the wilderness

Step by step is the way to freedom; if you walk with Me, it is certain
No reason for worry or anxiety, only true effort to climb the mountain
The 153 fish didn't leap into My disciples' boat; it required their action
After storing their catch, they had broken nets to mend and to maintain

A good work ethic is essential; nothing worthwhile comes on a platter
Find a labor of love or fill your work with love, and you build character

But you need My Spirit for wisdom and strength and trust in your Master
I Am always with you, paving the way wherever required in a new chapter

## April 25

## Don't Be My Constable

**2 Timothy 1:9**
*Who hath saved us, and called us with a holy calling, not according to our works, but according to his own purpose and grace, which was*
*given us in Christ Jesus before the world began.*

Emmanuel: God is with you; live in harmony, beauty, joy and happiness
Bless everyone in My name; pray for all to know My joy and goodness
Criticize no one, only desire their best; transformation is *My* business
Whether in conflict or with a desire to help, only pray for their progress

Why do My children become harsh and critical of people in trouble?
My Word is a two-edged sword; it's not to condemn but to be humble
Your Calling is to share My Love and Good News, not be My constable
Always share My Truth in Love; never forget to you I've been merciful

## April 26

## I Will Supply

**1 Peter 3:9**

*Not rendering evil for evil, or railing for railing: but contrariwise blessing;*
*knowing that ye are thereunto called, that ye should inherit a blessing.*

Deal with the slightest hint of fear by withdrawing into My Presence
If you are weary, take a break, wait till joy and strength are in balance
Fatigue and doubt lead to worry; I rested too, in My earthly existence
At Jacob's well, I relaxed before working My miracle for the Samaritans

Paul did all things in My strength; his Gentile mission had My blessing
Your spirit, not the body, should be the master of every undertaking
Often My purposes in the world are thwarted by initiatives well-meaning
By individuals driven by wrong motives that do not heed My warning

Endless work is not My Father's plan; at Cana we enjoyed a wedding
Renewal of spirit and physical rest, and for My disciples, some training

By changing water into wine, I gave marriage an exceptional meaning
My Mother's heart moved Me, and her concern for our host's standing

For all I ask you to do, I will supply you with strength and resources
Your Call is to live in Me, for Me, not to create My work experiences
I design your opportunities and give you the means and the choices
Don't bury talent, it leads to frustrating work in life; adds hindrances

# April 27

## Precious Gems

**Matthew 5:8**
*Blessed are the pure in heart: for they shall see God.*

You have never seen Me, but if you are faithful, you know I Am present
Do you feel disconnected from Me? Have you chosen to be disobedient?
If I appear to someone, it's not that the soul is spiritually elite or sentient
My visions are rare; if you don't receive an epiphany, do not be discontent

There are souls for whom I may span the physical and the spiritual realm
It may be to comfort or for a warning, or to rescue in a time of overwhelm
These are mysteries; I have many reasons; let it be, keep Me at the helm
Blessed are they who haven't seen yet believe, every one a precious gem

## April 28

## My Greatest Joy

**1 Corinthians 7:24**
*Brethren, let every man, wherein he is called, therein abide with God.*

I lead you through the wilderness; life is a journey I have planned
Up mountain heights, valleys, jungles, meadows, and the wasteland
How boring if all your experiences were pleasure filled and abundant
Bear your hardships patiently; wherever I lead, you will have My hand

Your Lord above is not like lords below; follow Me everywhere I show
Allow no vain fears to interfere or distress; overcome all, and you know
Hidden terrors cannot shake your breast: I Am in control of tomorrow
No threats can work their future woe; I've saved you from death's blow

I have given you talents, wisdom, and passion; how in life will you deploy?
Do you know that in *whatever* you do, there's a Calling for you in My employ?

Not a sacred secular disconnect, but your duty to witness against Satan's ploy
My Great Commission: it's My eternal quest to save souls, and My greatest joy

## April 29

## Move Your Mountain

**Matthew 21:21**
*Jesus answered and said unto them, Verily I say unto you,*
*If ye have faith, and doubt not, ye shall not only do this which Is*
*done to the fig tree, but also if ye shall say unto this mountain,*
*Be thou removed, and be thou cast into the sea; it shall be done.*

When life's challenges seem unbeatable, it may be dissonance
In My Kingdom, My grace is enough to overcome in obedience
Power, Love, Supply, everything is in perfection in My Presence
Lack of harmony, order, or success may indicate some imbalance

I haven't failed you when you feel deprived; learn how to obtain
My Word is a lamp and a light; it makes your path of life so plain
Hide it deep inside your heart, and throughout life, it will sustain
Your passage is well-lit; in My protection, now move the mountain

## April 30

## My Love, My Light

**Ecclesiastes 3:1**

*To every thing there is a season, and a time to every purpose under the heaven.*

Celebrate; there's no time like Spring; life awakes in everything
Cliff swallows migrate northward, confident I guide their wing
If you spent winter in discontent, it's time for your heart to sing
Hidden life waits to break forth underneath; reach for My blessing

Splendid Spring is My reassuring season for wintry hearts to delight
Still, if seeking warmth and shelter, know you are always in My sight
Fruit-bearing takes a while, but the promise of the blossoms is bright
Fear not; joy and wonder up ahead; My sunshine, My Love, My light

# May

## May 1

## My Wait Is Not a Veto

**Isaiah 30:18**
*And therefore will the Lord wait, that he may be gracious unto you,*
*and therefore will he be exalted, that he may have mercy upon you:*
*for the Lord is a God of judgment: blessed are all they that wait for him.*

My wait is not a veto; My stay is not a nay; My delay is not denial
In every hardship, you meet or path that closes, there is a tutorial
To discern eternal thought, learn your heavenly Father is impartial
Do not be discouraged by failure; I have the keys to your potential

Instant fulfillment is not the way of My Kingdom, even for a genius
Do not worry about waiting for a while; never in haste to be famous
Keep your conscience clear, engage in life joyfully within My radius
I don't hinder or deny you success; I Am your Guide, don't be anxious

There are situations where your life entwines with others in tandem
As urgent prayers constantly arrive for My instant approval at random

In those circumstances, it is not My reluctance to respond but wisdom
Every longing I must coordinate, for I know how you yearn for freedom

I Am your Maker; I Am your servant; My primary focus, your abundance
Every opportunity I seize to realize your aspirations under My guidance
To no hindrance do I ever concede in anything linked to your inheritance
There's always a dawn waiting for you, know I will slay all your dragons

## May 2

## The First Cause

**Genesis 1:1**
*In the beginning God created the heaven and the earth.*

Strive for peace with all, for no one will see the Lord without holiness
Relationships are significant challenges, causing difficulties and distress
Use difficult circumstances to conquer yourself, gaining in the process
"You shall be holy, for I Am holy." My Word the key to your happiness

Seek My Father's perfection; I urged My disciples as their assignment
It is not any less for you; abiding in Me secures your accomplishments
Your fears have no basis; it only takes a prayer; in Me, you are resilient
I Am the Alpha and the Omega; no power can snatch you, My instrument

Greek philosophers considered God the First Cause, quite a keen insight
Indeed, for I Am the source of everything in life that is good and right
The First Cause of birds and beasts, and rivers and seas, the day and night
Every color and beauty, and every man and woman to His utter delight

## May 3

## Get Rid of Self

**Matthew 6:14–15**

*For if ye forgive men their trespasses, your heavenly Father will also*
*forgive you: But if ye forgive not men their trespasses, neither will your Father forgive your trespasses.*

Getting rid of Self and any semblance of Pride is your vital lesson
Not only to depose Pride and Self but consign them to termination
Annihilate Self, make sure it's dead in the grave, not in suspension
Imprisoned Self is dangerous; it will sabotage your transformation

Replace the doomed Self with My loving Presence simultaneously
Celebrate death to Self and establish your new Life in Me jealously
You have exchanged your shallow Self-life for Mine, miraculously
Pardoned in My Love, observe My command, and forgive graciously

Remember how the Self in you would never forgive any offense?
That was a life of constant conflict; for you'd brook no grievance
Seeing every minor injury as major, losing My Power of forgiveness
That is the nature of Self; freedom comes by eliminating bitterness

You cannot forgive those who wrong you if dominated by Self-pride
As long as the Self can rear its ugly head, the poison lingers inside
Many do not understand; they feed their Self-life, thinking it died
Kill the Self; let go, let God; forgiving and forgetting, in Me abide

## May 4

## Come to Me

**Jeremiah 31:3**
*The Lord hath appeared of old unto me, saying, Yea, I have loved thee with an everlasting love therefore with loving kindness have I drawn thee.*

In My Love, joy and delight in the blessing and wonder of My Kingdom
Claim the extraordinary, not the humdrum, ask for help and My wisdom
And take up your life unafraid in peace and calm as you boldly overcome
You'll know I approve if you face your fears; work and live in My freedom

As a child in distress, you ran to your mother to show any bruises or pain
Whatever your needs you had or joys you shared, she would never disdain
Bring Me your successes and setbacks; I will look them over and explain
I Am your Maker; give Me the joy of providing your needs, in My domain

## May 5

## Leave It to Me

**John 4:24**

*God is a Spirit: and they that worship him must worship him in spirit and in truth.*

Worshipping Me in Spirit and Truth comes from the heart instinctively
My Love divine! No soul has explored the wondrous depths actively
The treasures in My coffers surpass what earth can provide entirely
And everything is yours; I can hardly wait to give you all completely

But pursue My humble life on earth; your inheritance is not uncertain
Through My death and Resurrection, Paradise reopened for your gain
Day by day, My grace confers all the resources you need in My domain
I set no limits; I only will the best for you, leave it all to Me as I sustain

## May 6

## I Haven't Forgotten

**Acts 4:20**

*For we cannot but speak the things which we have seen and heard.*

After the Fall, men ended up in a weary world of ceaseless labor
I came not in majesty but the flesh, as Son of man, humble Savior
And I give you rest and freedom in My Kingdom, your safe detour
Until I return, bear witness to the lost and weary, in faithful labor

"Come unto Me and I will give you rest," My yearning for all to listen
I have suffered; I can feel your pain and hardship; I haven't forgotten
Spirit-led, bold, and daring; share My Love and rest that you've gotten
Humbly serving with compassion, hear the cries of the lost and fallen

Tell them in My Love about the only hope for their eternal salvation
My poor world, I long for all to discover My tender loving care in union
Suffering in defiance, can you share to conquer My people's affliction?
Every soul is redeemable, none impossible; recall your transformation

## May 7

## Not Solitarily

**Deuteronomy 15:10**
*Thou shalt surely give him, and thine heart shall not be grieved when thou givest unto him: because that for this thing the Lord thy God shall bless thee in all thy works, and in all that thou puttest thine hand unto.*

If you are the haughty oarsman on your solo journey of life
There is peril in the river, swift currents, dangerously strong
The oarsman relying on Me trusts not wooden oars lifelong
I show the way against the tide, and he faithfully carries on

Did My disciples find the fish leaping into their boat readily?
They had to obey and cast their nets as they did regularly
You and I overcome life's hardships together, not solitarily
My blessing and honest effort; can succeed extraordinarily

## May 8

## In Life's Fray

**Hebrews 4:10**
*For he that is entered into his rest, he also hath ceased from his own works, as God did from his.*

Resting in Me often is the forgotten secret for a life-altering miracle
Make it a habit; trust and obey to see it can remove every obstacle
When I Am beside you; time stands still, for you are in My tabernacle
You venture into My realm where you can overcome even a debacle

Take things in stride, do one thing at a time; pause to relax and pray
I go ahead of you, follow Me, alert for My still, small voice every day
All of life is under My control; nothing to fear if you don't go astray
Remain in My Peace and Joy; be diligent but not driven, in life's fray

## May 9

## No Pedestals

**Romans 12:16**

*Be of the same mind one toward another. Mind not high things, but*
*condescend to men of low estate. Be not wise in your own conceits.*

Study the vanity of anyone mounted high on their arrogant pedestal
On the day of reckoning, the proud I will oppose; that bent is fatal
Power, Piety, Prestige, Perfection, and Pleasure can all be detrimental
Learn humility; haughtiness is rebellion; earthly wisdom is theoretical

Be discerning when you employ your knowledge, trust only My Word
Bring all matters small and large to My care, do not follow the herd
Who is wise and understanding? Many men's consciences are seared
My folly is wiser; My weakness stronger; than any human ability feared

Humility is following Me, not the Self; I chose the Cross, not My majesty
I disregarded My Power and Glory; I expect meekness from My devotee

With Pride comes shame and destruction for all those who are haughty
There is discord in the world; abide in Me and you will live in harmony

## May 10

## In Perfect Peace

**Isaiah 26:3**

*Thou wilt keep him in perfect peace, whose mind is stayed on thee: because he trusteth in thee.*

Anxiety is harmful; a calm spirit overcomes in any circumstance
You cannot destroy evil in haste; you must wait for My Guidance
Trust and obey; the battle belongs to Me, I Am alone your defense
Fear not and see My salvation, in perfect peace be in My Presence

When you have rest in Me, why would you allow any other condition?
Live and work in My tranquility, deliver your best efforts in any situation
In the world, speed is exalted; in My Kingdom, there is no competition
No need to hurry; My yoke is easy, My burden light and without tension

## May 11

## Include Me

**Psalm 25:4–5**

*Shew me thy ways, O LORD; teach me thy paths. Lead me in thy truth, and teach me: for thou art the God of my salvation; on thee do I wait all the day.*

In any relationship, you need My company; I will ensure concordance
Lover, relative, employer or friend, My Presence makes the difference
I release My Peace in unseen ways and put your difficulties in balance
Include Me, the Divine component, in all your relations; seek guidance

I Am the Great Shepherd; keep Me close, always be kind and humble
That mindset is what will help you make your relationships compatible
Know any partnership that excludes Me will eventually run into trouble
Listen to My advice, trust Me with life's alliances and keep them stable

## May 12

## Ride Out Every Storm

**Psalm 121:7–8**
*The LORD shall preserve thee from all evil: he shall preserve thy soul. The LORD shall preserve thy going out and thy coming in from this time forth, and even for evermore.*

Do not permit doubt and thoughts of trouble even for a second
Pick and choose your feelings like you would assess a diamond
Negative ideas rob your peace of mind like a devious vagabond
My Peace, Rest and Joy are the treasures that will never abscond

I have equipped you to face each day with My Love and laughter
You can ride out every storm; My protection is your safe harbor
Even the tempest is but a lesson; learn from it and build character
All is well, no matter how alarming the reading from the barometer

## May 13

## Only I Can Heal

**Matthew 28:19**

*Go ye therefore, and teach all nations, baptizing them in the name of*
*the Father, and of the Son, and of the Holy Ghost.*

I have commanded you to influence the world in My Great Commission
But if you are to teach and impact others, Self-conquest is a precondition
The mandate is to disciple people, not control them or flaunt your position
In Aramaic "Go, therefore, make Talmidim," was "Disciples" in translation

I was hard on the Pharisees; ordinary people knew I was kind and humble
Sinners felt safe; to tax collectors, hookers, and lepers, I was accessible
For all My needy people, would you be compassionate or act intractable?
I was humiliated and spat upon, so may you; for My sake, be vulnerable

Judge no one, even your enemies, remember "Father forgive," My appeal
To make disciples, bear no malice; point men to Me; learn from My ordeal

I designed the human heart; I know its complexity, and I alone can reveal
Sin creates doubt, hardship, pain, and despair; such agony only I can heal

## May 14

## Reckless Lover

**Romans 5:8**
*But God commendeth his love toward us, in that, while we were yet sinners, Christ died for us.*

I delight in intimacy, especially when you demand with confidence
That gives Me the right to state My requirements, too, in congruence
Doesn't a child's claim on parents prove love and freedom in evidence?
Our relationship grows in tenderness and trust by abiding in My Presence

I Am the Great Lover courting you in the Song of Solomon; I Am reckless
My Love is not just about My grace and compassion but your happiness
God dwells in you; My Father and I are one; thence, our Love is endless
Divinity in you calls for perfection, like your heavenly Father in holiness

Not everyone is identical on the spiritual plane in motives or aspiration
Like those who may not want to share your motives or your aspiration

You are the temple of God; My Holy Spirit confirms your transformation
Keep this in mind, and try to understand others in your daily interaction

## May 15

## Material Frustration

**Ephesians 3:19**
*And to know the love of Christ, which passeth knowledge, that ye might be filled with all the fulness of God.*

When you focus on your material desires, you end in frustration
A spirit being you are clothed in flesh, it is a temporary condition
Man's ambition exceeds spiritual primacy with eternal ramifications
Lack of supply is usually the lack of belief; it is a spiritual situation

To secure physical needs, step up, don't neglect the Spiritual domain
Seek My Kingdom and My righteousness, trusting that you will obtain
Do not worry, fret and fuss; provision from My storehouse is certain
Journey into a deeper faith and trust and believe My Love will sustain

In striving for the riches of My Kingdom, there's no cause for concern
My plans and purposes you learned; apply, and your life let Me govern
You are not robots; My gift of your free will gives you power to discern
To know the difference between right and wrong, My Word, your lantern

## May 16

## Pray and Praise

**John 15:7**

*If ye abide in me, and my words abide in you, ye shall ask what ye will,*
*and it shall be done unto you.*

How can you gain strength and peace if trust isn't your disposition?
If asked, I will grant power, but Pride often stands in the situation
Those not humble enough to accept My help end up having tension
Pray ceaselessly, never weary, make abiding in Me your resolution

One day you will know I answered all your prayers so wondrously
And deeply regret that you did not communicate more consciously
Spontaneous or standard, in cathedrals, or men's hearts, faithfully
Prayer builds a bedrock of gold, silver, or precious stones gloriously

Steadfast prayer is an exercise; habituate it with Praise; it doesn't strain
Challenges cleared one by one in your slate when My grace you obtain

Your great mountains, cares and concerns, heartaches, trials, and pains
Prayer changes all; it recreates and reassures if you hand Me the reins

## May 17

## Valiant in Faith

**John 16:22**

*And ye now therefore have sorrow: but I will see you again, and your*
*heart shall rejoice, and your joy no man taketh from you.*

Hardships, heartaches, and sorrows no longer control your fate
It may seem like nothing goes right when challenges accelerate
My valiant in Faith know My joy in the morning, they anticipate
The night will pass because their Savior took the sinner's place

## May 18

## Look at Me

**Isaiah 45:22**

*Look unto me, and be ye saved, all the ends of the earth: for I Am God, and there is none else.*

My salvation promise is based not on merit; it is for all who glance
That may sound incredible, but all the ends of the earth get a chance
All one needs to do is *look* at Me; immediately obtain My assurance
But free will is within everyone's power; and many keep their distance

Moses' brass serpent on a stake, heeded, gave life though it was lifeless
Turn to Me with your eye of Faith, you'll be saved from all your distress
Look to Me for My Peace that passes all understanding, and you possess
Fix your gaze on Me, exchange doubt, for Joy, eternal life, and happiness

## May 19

## Safe Harbor

**Psalm 107:29**
*He maketh the storm a calm, so that the waves thereof are still.*

If your life is driven it indicates mistrust, perhaps an illness
You're safe in My hands; show Me your Faith makes progress
My ship of salvation sails stormy seas; it is never rudderless
I Am your servant-Captain leading you on to eternal success

Are you sure I can save you even if you fall into the ocean?
Drowning in the Atlantic, Indian, Pacific, or Mediterranean?
Without certainty, you'll despair, believe you have no Guardian
Many call Me Lord, doubt My Word, and claim to be Christian

Storms and tempests are not the sum of life; I Am, your Savior
When the voyage on life's vessel is rough, I Am the safe harbor
I Am the Master of the sea, of nature's might and its behavior
Fear not, I'll guide you to heaven's shores, secure in My favor

## May 20

## Never Conquered

**2 Timothy 1:7**

*For God hath not given us the spirit of fear; but of power, and of love, and of a sound mind.*

I have given you a Spirit of Power and Love; no force can conquer
No matter how great your challenges may be, I will always shelter
You will triumph with My Presence, though you may feel shattered
All evil I will vanquish; trust and overcome even if you are battered

## May 21

## Not an Option

**Revelation 3:5**

*He that overcometh, the same shall be clothed in white raiment; and I will not blot his name out of the book of life, but I will confess his name before my Father, and before his angels.*

Worries weigh you down, keeping life in constant turbulence
Trust Me with all your woes, or you won't know My Presence
If My face is hidden, it's because your fears are disobedience
Giving Me your burdens is vital for your spiritual inheritance

Obedience brings forth My wisdom and grace; it is not an option
I paid the penalty for your sins; in Me is your life and Resurrection
Your role is to trust; faithfully obey Me to work out your salvation
Good works cannot save you, but they prove your transformation

Overcoming sin is impossible; My help and your obedience is essential
Apart from Me, you can do nothing to will or act for My purposes crucial
Wherever I may lead you, I will sustain you with My grace and approval
Share My Love across the seas or at home till I celebrate your safe arrival

## May 22

## Royal Position

**Romans 8:16–17**

*The Spirit itself beareth witness with our spirit, that we are the children*
*of God: And if children, then heirs; heirs of God, and joint-heirs with*
*Christ; if so be that we suffer with him, that we may be also glorified together.*

Trust is of two kinds; one brooks no delay, and one will wait patiently
The first, sure of My purpose and guidance demands I approve promptly
Persisting like a child pleading urgency, and it touches My heart directly
The other I will favor no less; for its perseverance moves Me differently

I Am your true friend; all I have is yours by right; I Am at your command
Serving in My Kingdom, you are family; heirs have privileges to demand
But don't wait till your supply runs out; make your claim well beforehand
Don't ask as a supplicant; as joint heirs to My inheritance, take your stand

It is not the privilege of all who call Me Lord, Lord and choose rebellion

Only those just, merciful, and humble with evidence of transformation
My princes in Sonship can freely impose because of your royal position
No question of waiting outside My palace in apprehensive supplication

## May 23

## Why I Insist

**1 Corinthians 7:32**
*But I would have you without carefulness.*

Little fears and anxieties pile up if you allow them to persist
Until you get that sorted out with Me from all work, desist
Harboring them is disobeying My will; that is why I insist
Bring Me what disturbs you; in My service, it cannot exist

Promptly communicate when My assignments are all executed
Manage My resources well; faithfulness, not results, get inspected
Rejoice after duty gets done; then, you can do more when granted
The outcome is not your responsibility once work gets completed

## May 24

## My Modus Operandi

**Psalm 96:3**
*Declare his glory among the heathen, his wonders among all people.*

Do you feel nobody knows or cares about your joys and sorrows?
Life passes you by, unknown and ignored; you live in the shadows
But there is One who numbers the hairs on your head; He follows
Your heartaches, struggles and victories, and all your tomorrows

Freely you received, freely give; let every soul know their Redeemer
You are in the palm of My hands; guide the wounded to My shelter
They must obtain what you have; My Love can shape their character
Lead more and more to Me; tell them waiting for them is their Savior

What if you were a disciple handing out food to feed the five thousand
You pass on the loaves of bread and fish, as they multiply in your hand
Observing all My disciples, I was studying what they would understand
Did My miracle include Faith in sharing, or only My prayer and command?

Believing there wasn't enough food could have created an impediment
I wanted them to trust and share and have a role in all the amazement
That's how things work in My Kingdom; you believe; I Am management
Abundance is My modus operandi; take, but apportion all the enjoyment

## May 25

## Go and Flourish

**Mark 4:31–32**

*It is like a grain of mustard seed, which, when it is sown in the earth,*
*Is less than all the seeds that be in the earth: But when it is sown, it*
*groweth up, and becometh greater than all herbs, and shooteth out*
*great branches; so that the fowls of the air may lodge under the shadow of it.*

Realize, in My will, there is nothing that you cannot accomplish
Never give up on a task because it seems impossible to finish
Confirm its obedience to My Word; then go ahead and flourish
I will honor all you do; the best is a labor of love you cherish

The Kingdom of God is like a mustard seed someone has planted
Pushing through soil with no certainty, it takes nothing for granted
Compelled by its Maker, completes its task and grows as cultivated
Smallest of herbs, it sprouts great branches; shelters birds delighted

## May 26

## Spiritual Training

**Isaiah 58:10–11**

*And if thou draw out thy soul to the hungry, and satisfy the afflicted*
*soul; then shall thy light rise in obscurity, and thy darkness be as the*
*noon day: And the Lord shall guide thee continually, and satisfy thy*
*soul in drought, and make fat thy bones: and thou shalt be like a*
*watered garden, and like a spring of water, whose waters fail not.*

Material blessings do not indicate that spiritual life is thriving
The assumption is common but is not essential biblical thinking
It's the ability to trust with no outward evidence of My blessing
"Though He slay me yet will I trust Him," said Job of God's testing

Store up treasures in heaven; focusing on wealth creates tension
Lack of supply and lack of belief may indicate a spiritual condition
Spiritual disciplines are essential: Bible study, prayer and meditation
Giving to the poor, mercy, humility, all these have a direct correlation

You meet people remarkably demonstrating My Power as evidence
Consider their commitment; it precedes their ability and influence

Discipline is vital; spiritual growth is not a double minded existence
Spiritually trained, you can't fail to help others gain their inheritance

## May 27

## Be Grounded

**Matthew 5:13**
*Ye are the salt of the earth: but if the salt has lost his savour, wherewith shall it be salted? it is thenceforth good for nothing, but to be cast out, and to be trodden under foot of men.*

There are two aspects of growth: the hidden root and the open shoot
Without being rooted, the plant cannot flower nor produce any fruit
You, too, must be grounded in Me or life and work will be destitute
Like salt without flavor, without My Power, you cannot contribute

## May 28

## The Power of My Love

**Acts 3:19**

*Repent ye therefore, and be converted, that your sins may be blotted out,*
*when the times of refreshing shall come from the presence of the Lord.*

Ours is no ordinary love story; I died and rose to love you eternally
Know that in every struggle, trial, or defeat, I Am with you constantly
Can you prove My Presence is enough for you by living confidently?
If fears can still overcome you, pray to know My Love more deeply

## May 29

## In Oblivion

**Ephesians 2:4–5**

*But God, who is rich in mercy, for his great love wherewith he loved us,*
*Even when we were dead in sins, hath quickened us together with Christ*
*(by grace ye are saved).*

Past, Present and Future; your sins and failures I flung into oblivion
Trust Me in this issue, have no fear; all your iniquities I have forgiven
Viewing nature's beauty from peaks, a mountaineer forgets pollution
Breathe in My daily blessings; My mercies are new every morning

I designed you to bear a twenty-four-hour burden; to it, add nothing
Not the years before nor even the days ahead; that has no meaning
Your past, I have erased; that burden, don't foolishly start reloading
You mock Me if you expect Me to haul it or want Me to be carrying

Walk with Me one day at a time; joyful to see what I have provided
Ask for strength day by day; travel light; you mustn't be overloaded

No soldier carries useless baggage to war, but only what is needed
My Word will keep your mind and spiritual life guarded; undefeated

# May 30

## Mighty Prayer

**Isaiah 54:17**

*No weapon that is formed against thee shall prosper; and every tongue*
*that shall rise against thee in judgment thou shalt condemn.*

Merely accepting, being resigned to My Will, cannot vanquish evil
One method, made a habit, unleashes My Spirit power that indwells
The heart praising Me in all circumstances is the devil's death knell
So Pray, employing Praise as a weapon to destroy the devilry of Hell

And here is another little secret of making Joy an everyday experience
Turn your eyes upon Me throughout the day; it will make a difference
My Love, your security, and the thrill at the nearness of My Presence
All your fears will vanish; nothing to impede success with My guidance

## May 31

## How to Pray

**Jeremiah 33:3**
*Call unto me, and I will answer thee, and shew thee great and mighty things, which thou knowest not.*

Prayer need not be boring, uninteresting, tiring, always kneeling
Make it engaging, compelling, thought-provoking, and refreshing
You need both your friends and Me for your health and well-being
Spare a thought or two for Me in the day; for I Am always waiting

You have so many ways to interact; I designed you to communicate
A flash of Faith, a caring word, a heart of grit, all of them I appreciate
No need always to speak; I know what you need; relax and celebrate
What if you sin or fail? Come to Me, your loving, merciful magistrate

# June

## June 1

## Divine Longing

**Matthew 8:11**

*And I say unto you, That many shall come from the east and west, and*
*shall sit down with Abraham, and Isaac, and Jacob, in the kingdom of heaven.*

Be consumed by My Love; only then can you know divine communion
To live My Love is to be seized by the Joy and wonderment of our union
But "Whom the Lord loveth He chasteneth." Be prepared for correction
Living is thinking of Me often, communicating, seeking My transformation

The source of Divine Love is My tremendous longing to restore humanity
You have to live your Love in deeds, not only in words; I chose mortality
For man's salvation, I suffered, died, and resurrected; I took responsibility
I expect nothing more from you than to trust and obey to become like Me

# June 2

## My Image

**Daniel 3:24–25**

*Then Nebuchadnezzar the king was astonished, and rose up in haste, and*
*spake, and said unto his counsellors, Did not we cast three men bound into*
*the midst of the fire? They answered and said unto the king, True, O king.*
*He answered and said, Lo, I see four men loose, walking in the midst of the*
*fire, and they have no hurt; and the form of the fourth is like the Son of God.*

Recognize My Love in everything I've given you; I've given you everything
Every breath you draw is My gift; do you doubt when life is disappointing?
Trials and challenges are to help you change and give life more meaning
Moses couldn't see My face, nor you; can you bear My image in suffering?

You can't get scorched in the crucible of My Love; I Am with you in the fire
As I was with Shadrach, Meshach, and Abednego, in Babylon's great empire
Not even their clothes singed in the furnace of Nebuchadnezzar king-umpire
But the Self must wither and die, for you must be like Me; that is My desire

## June 3

## Love Is Fruitful

**2 Thessalonians 1:3**
*We are bound to thank God always for you, brethren, as it is meet, because that your faith groweth exceedingly, and the charity of every*
*one of you all toward each other aboundeth.*

I loved them all—publicans, sinners, harlots, making no exception
Exclude no one; if you love Me, follow Me; make no differentiation
Love as a weapon drives out sin with the power of My transformation
Fear, sadness, and failure go if you employ Praise in every condition

What is Praise but grateful acceptance of My love and resources
Would you give more gifts to someone who never even notices?
Hence Praise with a thankful heart; you will receive My promises
Gratitude transcends common courtesy—one of the best practices

It's not about your satisfaction every day but always being thankful
It's about receiving My loving provisions and always being faithful
It's not about counting your blessings but sharing; in My Love, fruitful
It's about praising Me in good times and bad, your heart always joyful

## June 4

## I Will See You Through

**John 6:28–29**

*Then said they unto him, What shall we do, that we might work the works of God? Jesus answered and said unto them, This is the work of God, that ye believe on him whom he hath sent.*

I chasten those I Love; but it is your work, recognizing your wrong motives or desires is a job for everyone
Bring every deed and thought to Me, and your work gets done
For all your sins and failures, I paid the price; your guilt is gone

But failings realized cause pain and frustration that are a residue
As you grow in Faith, you discover changes were long overdue
Weaknesses you overlooked with no sorrow now make you stew
Fear not; take courage in your heart and be glad; I Am with you

Your feelings indicate progress; slow perhaps but have patience
That is how you gain compassion for others and more tolerance
Overcoming hardship, troubles, and failures needs perseverance
Keep going; don't give up; I will see you through this experience

## June 5

### Tender Power

**1 Peter 5:7**
*Casting all your anxieties on him, because he cares for you.*

Mine is the still, small voice, listen to it; ignore the world's cacophony
Tenderly I call, listen to Me, give me all discouragement and acrimony
Abide in Me and rest, not in My Power but in My Peace and harmony
In My tenderness and rest, you find healing to overcome your agony

I attend to your wounds, heal, and make you strong in My loving care
You are never left helpless at the world's mercy; My Power you share
My Angels guard you day and night; nothing can harm you; I Am there
From dangers unseen I shield you; for without Me you would despair

# June 6

## Yours Personally

**Deuteronomy 28:8**

*The LORD shall command the blessing upon thee in thy storehouses, and in all that thou settest thine hand unto; and he shall bless thee in the land which the LORD thy God giveth thee.*

Don't see Me as others do; men's needs differ; relate to Me uniquely
Whether it's Church, My disciples, or My followers, I work specifically
Understand My supply for everyone's needs gets distributed personally
Trust My mercies are new every day, and My grace is yours abundantly

When you are weak, My strength is yours; when strong, My tenderness
Tempted, fallen, you need My salvation; if righteous, learn My kindness
When you are lonely, you need My company; and to fight sin, My fortress
Can anyone but your Savior God fit the role? I will lead you to success

## June 7

## My Kingdom's Riches

**Matthew 6:20–21**

*But lay up for yourselves treasures in heaven, where neither moth nor rust doth corrupt, and where thieves do not break through nor steal: For where your treasure is, there will your heart be also.*

Grow in the beauty of holiness and live with My grace and power
Forever reaching for resources of My Kingdom in your character
Notice how the very form of an animal alters in feeding behavior
You, too, transform, obtaining My treasures, seeing their wonder

My Kingdom's riches of gold, silver, and precious gems last forever
Not mined from earth like the stones pursued by every entrepreneur
These are the treasures in every man's heart that lead to your Savior
My Word is a lamp giving you My light and salvation's eternal armor

## June 8

## The Only Way

**1 Peter 5:8**
*Be sober, be vigilant; because your adversary the devil, as a roaring lion, walketh about, seeking whom he may devour.*

My Power keeps millions of souls from being hunted like prey
The Faith of your fathers endures persecution to this very day
Despite dungeon, fire and sword, My soldiers persist and pray
Your hopes stay alive not in comfort but trusting Me every day

This holy Faith is not for the flesh but the soul; choose correctly
I consent only to what is best for the soul, for My eternal family
Yield to My Word, radical change results; life transforms sublimely
Rejecting it frustrates My intent, impedes your prayers adversely

Your spiritual pace slows, and regret binds heart and conscience
Half-hearted promises make life a struggle, making no difference
For the only assurance you need is in Me; I will give you guidance
I'll wipe clean all the debt you acquired with My grace and Presence

The heart's paradox may be puzzling, but the evidence is compelling
Enslaved to sinful instincts, powerless without Me, you need My healing

Heaven's ladder seems high; don't trust yourself; submit to My training
Scarred but healed of moral wounds, you will be thrilled to be sharing

## June 9

## Finish the Race

**Hebrews 12:1**

*Wherefore seeing we also are compassed about with so great a cloud of*
*witnesses, let us lay aside every weight, and the sin which doth so easily*
*beset us, and let us run with patience the race that is set before us.*

What would you think of a runner starting a race who gives up at once
Remembering his failures, he believes he cannot go the long distance
Life is an obstacle course; I designed you to overcome with resilience
Conquer your fears and hardships; you do not run alone in My Presence

This race is not only to obtain your heart's desires; it is Me you will gain
My Joy will lift you above all your doubts if in Me you constantly remain
Low valleys or steep mountaintops, run towards Me, I will never disdain
Discard a sense of failure; bounce back when you fall; trust Me to maintain

## June 10

## Secret of Supply

**Psalm 50:14–16**

*Offer unto God thanksgiving; and pay thy vows unto the most High:*
*And call upon me in the day of trouble: I will deliver thee, and thou shalt glorify me.*

A thankful heart knows the secret of fulfilling its vows and promises
Investments in My Bank of Heaven guarantee funds for all expenses
Whenever a need arises, there's no need to worry, even in your crises
The uninitiated will envy; how do you get provision for your damages?

What they overlook is small deposits of faithful work made in obedience
The man of Faith claims his right; demands funds from his bank balance
Ignorant, untrained eyes see magic; but he's only claiming his inheritance
Promises he kept; there's no hocus pocus in My policy of Divine Insurance

My children offer Praise as a sacrifice constantly, thanking My holy name
Study the lives of My saints; in situations great and small, they overcame

Store your little acts of faithfulness in My storehouse until it's time to claim
Trust Me in everything; in your time of need, I will never put you to shame

I promise I'll see you through trials; pass through water, douse every fire
Fear nothing; I forgave your sins; explore My will and ask for all you desire
Faith can move mountains; look for no other solutions if situations are dire
My Death and Resurrection is your story of freedom, key to all you require

## June 11

### Perpetual Peace

**Exodus 14:14**
*The Lord shall fight for you, and ye shall hold your peace.*

There is a Peace that passes all understanding man cannot understand
It is My Peace needed in a worried, stressed-out world that I didn't plan
To know that Peace, citizenship is a requirement in My Kingdom for man
It is the mark of your Lord and Savior, Jesus Christ; it's only for My clan

My Peace doesn't change or fade with life's daily pressures; it is stable
It empowers you to discern the world's values, but you must be humble
Resides deep in your heart; so nothing can overcome you in any crucible
Like nothing else you can ever find, it is My Promise of Love, perpetual

# June 12

## Heavenly Home

**John 14:1–2**

*Let not your heart be troubled: ye believe in God, believe also in me.*
*In my Father's house are many mansions: if it were not so, I would have told you. I go to prepare a place for you.*

Listen for My Voice, be vigilant; the great sign of Faith is obedience
Many call Me Lord, Lord, but do not obey; that is not true allegiance
That's like building your house on sand; razed in the storm's violence
But only a wise man who erects on rock knows it makes a difference

Living My Sermon on the Mount, faithfully keep My commandments
My intimate followers obey Me implicitly with their total commitment
Each soul personally hears My Word as I give guidance; I Am patient
Your bedrock is built stone by stone, obedience, the main component

I Am the rock in your Home of Obedience, your unshakable foundation
In many faithful homes, I dwell gladly with My children of every nation

Every house constructed with mortar of My Word and humble adoration
With an anchor for every tempest, living in safety under My protection

But one day you'll dwell in your heavenly home with your dear Savior
No more tears nor toiling, no sorrow nor pain, and no more hard labor
With angels and saints, you'll worship joyfully in all heavenly splendor
Reigning with the Holy Trinity, praising your home of beauty and power

## June 13

## Not by Might

**Zechariah 4:6**
*Then he answered and spake unto me, saying, This is the word of the Lord unto Zerubbabel, saying, Not by might, nor by power, but by my spirit, saith the Lord of hosts.*

Life is a mountaineering expedition; sometimes, the climb is steep
In your journey, obstacles can make you doubt; or make you weep
If you conclude they're impossible to beat; you give up, fall asleep
But trust Me, I can use you if, in Faith, you will try and take a leap

Conquer your challenges; know that you are not alone in your climb
I haven't given you a spirit of fear, but Power, Love, and a Sound Mind
Tell the world My death and Resurrection have changed the paradigm
Step out in Faith; see what waits beyond the mountain; now's the time!

Overcoming your obstacles, you can now help others with confidence
My Love is for sharing, not hoarding; help many gain their inheritance

Kingdom work is not by might; it is My Spirit that makes the difference
Whatever you choose to do, if you do it for Me, it has My acceptance

# June 14

## New Birth

**Ezekiel 11:19**

*And I will give them one heart, and I will put a new spirit within you;*
*and I will take the stony heart out of their flesh, and will give them an*
*heart of flesh.*

Usually, it is not the situation; it is you that first needs to change
When that genuinely happens, things fall into place and rearrange
Make every attempt to be like Me, don't become someone strange
A different kind of person from before, new inside out, born again

Put away every thought of failure, make a fresh start in My Name
Do your best one day at a time; fear not, I took away your shame
I Am all you need; count on Me for guidance, for I will never blame
There's so much you can do in My Kingdom, only do not seek fame

## June 15

## My Promises

**Revelation 3:12**

*Him that overcometh will I make a pillar in the temple of my God, and*
*he shall go no more out: and I will write upon him the name of my God,*
*and the name of the city of my God, which is new Jerusalem, which cometh*
*down out of heaven from my God: and I will write upon him my new name.*

The wonders I Am planning for you are beyond your understanding
Oh! How I long for you to realize My Grace and Mercy never-ending
The awe of being under My wings may register but are you abiding?
My Holy Spirit lives inside of you; a faithful life is your great Calling

Count all things worthless, consider Me your solitary authentic gain
My steadfast Love never ceases, bringing Joy, soothing your pain
A new era in your life has dawned; ask what you will, and you obtain
I astonish overcomers; know all My promises are genuine and certain

## June 16

## Struggles Cease

**1 John 5:5**
*Who is he that overcometh the world, but he that believeth that Jesus is the Son of God?*

When you are mine, no evil can overcome; trust in My assurance
Do not fear; trust Me as we walk together, safe in My Presence
Like two friends meeting, for the loving friendship they experience
Rest in Me not only when stressed but come for perfect guidance

You'd always be at ease if you spent more time with Me constantly
But My children show up only in trouble when they're full of anxiety
Unaware many hardships wouldn't arise if they sought Me frequently
Always be as eager to see Me just as when difficulties arise promptly

When you abide in My unshakable Peace, burdens are easy to release
You obtain the strength to conquer challenges, and problems decrease
Whatever comes your way, there's a calm serenity as struggles cease
Seek Me and find Me early, long before life's daily demands increase

## June 17

## My Holy Name

**Acts 4:12**
*Neither is there salvation in any other: for there is none other name under heaven given among men, whereby we must be saved.*

There is no other name remembered on earth than "Jesus"
People often use My Name in ways disrespectful, frivolous
They do not realize what they are doing could be serious
Uzzah touched the Ark, and he died for being spontaneous

Moses, I denied entry to the Promised Land for disobedience
He struck the rock when speaking to it was My requirement
Today My mercies are new every morning in My New Covenant
Careless use of My Name is permitted; there's no punishment

But what blasphemers do not know is that there is a reason
I allow global, frequent use of My Holy Name with no reaction
When I return, none can claim ignorance or lack of information
For I Am the only God mocked even in casual communication

My children, I will set you on high, for you know My Name
Your Prophet, Priest and King, I died, and I took your shame
Tread underfoot the forces of evil; your Savior, I proclaim
Jesus Christ of Nazareth, your inheritance, you gladly claim

# June 18

## A Life Apart

**Deuteronomy 5:13**
*Six days thou shalt labour, and do all thy work.*

Constant activity cannot dominate a life of genuine service
That is the world's way, not mine; in Me, you rest and rejoice
More than busyness, a life of prayer and obedience will suffice
Take on extra work only when I instruct; make that your practice

The world boasts of self-made men; that should not be your aim
Such individuals labor not for Me but power, riches, and fame
In your service for My Kingdom, challenges you face are not tame
But you will know you accomplished My will and indeed overcame

## June 19

## Two Keys

**1 Kings 2:3**

*And keep the charge of the LORD thy God, to walk in his ways, to keep his statutes, and his commandments, and his judgments, and his testimonies, as it is written in the law of Moses, that thou mayest*
*prosper in all that thou doest, and whithersoever thou turnest thyself.*

Obedience and humility are paths that lead to your heavenly Father
What is your treasure, material success or My Kingdom to further?
Or will you diligently seek My spiritual wonders to take you higher
The blessed fruit of the Holy Spirit to fill your heart and soul forever

For now, you work in the material plane; to meet your responsibilities
There is no sacred-secular divide in My Kingdom; both are the keys
Employ them together in perfect balance, and they will lead to Me
My promise or My command, follow Me, faithful in trust and humility

## June 20

## My Presence

**Hebrews 11:6**
*But without faith it is impossible to please him: for he that cometh to God must believe that he is, and that he is a rewarder of them that diligently seek him.*

Discern My will in all things and at any cost, obey
I freed you from what could have kept you a slave
Fear not; whenever you are in trouble, I will save
I Am your refuge and your strength; My life I gave

You long to see Me face to face in the flesh, visible
See Me with eyes of Faith; My Presence is tangible
I wait to see you, too; bless you and work a miracle
The problem is—I cannot if you think it's impossible

## June 21

## Trust And See

**John 17:3**

*And this is life eternal, that they might know thee the only true God, and Jesus Christ, whom thou hast sent.*

Only by abiding in Me, not by reason or study, can you have My mind
The mind of Jesus Christ; then you will learn of Me, and you will find
That I walk with you, I Am your God, and you share in My life divine
Obey My decrees, believe, though your eyes see only bread and wine

Wonders unfold in My Presence; come to Me, the source of all happiness
For unsurpassed Peace and inner quiet, hope renewed and My forgiveness
With every blessing and Joy, protected from all tempests in My fortress
I Am your only Hope, the Way, the Truth, and Life in a world of distress

## June 22

## Your Red Sea

**Exodus 14:28–29**

*And the waters returned, and covered the chariots, and the horsemen, and all the host of Pharaoh that came into the sea after them; there remained not so much as one of them. But the children of Israel walked upon dry land in the midst of the sea; and the waters were a wall unto them on their right hand, and on their left.*

I led them out of Egypt, be sure I will tear apart your Red Sea
You may not have come to it yet; it lies ahead; walk fearlessly
Dangers lurk not only in the deep; other obstacles are deadly
Nothing can stop you from the Promised Land; you are with Me

When you come to a place with no way out, no hope of escape
If you are ready to give up, look for the gap only I can shape
I may escalate the wind or blot the sun with a curtain I drape
Your fears I will dismiss and mock your enemies as they gape

## June 23

## Sit by My Well

**John 4:14**
*But whosoever drinketh of the water that I shall give him shall never thirst; but the water that I shall give him shall be in him a well of water springing up into everlasting life.*

Ask of Me, and I will give you living water to revive your spirit
My Divine life flows into you when you abide in Me; you inherit
Weary, I sat by Jacob's Well; but its water by itself had no merit
I Am the gift of Life the Samaritan woman obtained, to her credit

When tired and thirsty in life's journey, know I Am the Living Water
Challenges will appear on the horizon, and your Faith may falter
Troubled and discouraged, your soul daunted, bring Me the matter
Stay with Me a while; rested and refreshed, you build your character

# June 24

## Calm and Secure

**Job 11:19**
*Also thou shalt lie down, and none shall make thee afraid; yea, many shall make suit unto thee.*

Do not delay when I instruct; only wait if you receive no guidance
Calmly engage your duties faithfully, quietly, with no disturbance
That is Faith at work, deserving of My reward for your obedience
I love to see you calm and secure; your trust in Me is the evidence

## June 25

## Divine Lover

**Psalm 61:7**
*He shall abide before God for ever: O prepare mercy and truth, which may preserve him.*

I Am no ordinary friend; your woes and fears only I can transform
True earthly friends are rare; in My Love, you'll ride out any storm
Need a break on life's busy highway? Hide in My sheltered platform
In Me alone is Sabbath calm; for minds and hearts, it's a gentle balm

Place all your hopes in Me; no one else could ever love you more
Do you reflect on the wonder of our relationship, or do you ignore
Earthly kings rarely meet subjects without an appointment before
But you can summon your God and Creator anytime to your door

In need, morning, noon, and night, instantly call for My Presence
Share your deep longings, hurts, and fears, don't keep a distance
Men awed by creation, fear, and tremble in mindless ritual reverence
Your Savior, Lord, Divine Lover's adoration—is intimate experience

# June 26

## Little Things

**Proverbs 21:5**

*The thoughts of the diligent tend only to plenteousness; but of everyone that is hasty only to want.*

Hustling and bustling is not the way you implement My guidance
Delay the pressures of daily life; wait until you have My assurance
Poise is essential; for both small and big decisions need patience
Small things count, seeking help only in crucial work lacks diligence

Do not get impatient doing what is simple; I do not scorn little things
I created great mountains, seas and flowers, tiny hummingbird wings
The blazing sun, the snowflake, the Blue Whale, Bumble Bee that stings
You, too, with My grace and loving care, can excel in all the little things

## June 27

## No Self-Reproach

**Psalm 27:5**

*For in the time of trouble he shall hide me in his pavilion: in the secret of his tabernacle shall he hide me; he shall set me up upon a rock.*

Not the palsied sinner, the Samaritan, nor the trapped adulteress
None did I condemn to bear the burden of sinful consciousness
Learn of Me in loving your fellow man; only then can you witness
And run to obtain your prize; your Faith in Me crowns your success

So claim My shelter as a Kingdom life seeker, spiritually soaring
Rising above earth-life, unburdened by failures, you are growing
Higher in Faith and Hope, over the clouds, keep on ascending
Taking every step in My Word, a lamp to your feet illuminating

# June 28

## Dwell Forever

**Psalm 23:6**
*Surely goodness and mercy shall follow me all the days of my life: and I will dwell in the house of the LORD forever.*

My teaching and training you will never be in vain
Consider restraint, obstacles, and hardship are all gain
When I change your woe to wonder, you will exclaim!
To give you My Life in abundance is the reason I came

Your life will flood through with joy and gladness
At My table of delight, you will lose your sadness
Your sins forgiven, burdens mine, with all distress
Feast on My blessings, My Love, and My goodness

I Am your Savior; trust Me to change you and know
From the bottom of your heart, your cup will overflow
Expect that My goodness and mercy will forever follow
You will dwell with your Lord in His eternal bungalow

## June 29

## I Will Fend

**2 Timothy 4:18**
*And the Lord shall deliver me from every evil work, and will preserve*
*me unto his heavenly kingdom: to whom be glory for ever and ever. Amen.*

So complete is My Love and care for you; you'll never lose My hold
Evil cannot overcome you; I'll bless your circumstances and uphold
First, be convinced it's for your best and trust that I do not withhold
The Father and I are one; all things are possible in My Power, behold

I know all your struggles; I can see the road far ahead; its every bend
You cannot see nor bear the future, leave it all to Me, and I will fend
Life's storms and trials are part of your journey; in My grace contend
When it seems more than you can take, remember I Am your Friend

## June 30

## Never Shame

**John 13:34–35**

*A new commandment I give unto you, That ye love one another; as I have loved you, that ye also love one another. By this shall all men know that ye are my disciples, if ye have love one to another.*

Share My Joy and the abundant blessings you have received
So much you obtained, much more to come; you are so loved
Love in return breaks the barriers; building walls is depraved
Understanding, kindness, and mercy can change all enslaved

To Me, you do belong; love all in your heavenly Father's Name
Red, yellow, black, and white are precious in My sight; the same
It is for the dull, tiresome, sinful, critical, and miserable I came
I made you in My image; bless all; never put anyone to shame

# July

## July 1

## Speak My Word

**Galatians 2:16**

*Knowing that a man is not justified by the works of the law, but by the faith of Jesus Christ, even we have believed in Jesus Christ, that we might be justified by the faith of Christ, and not by the works of the law: for by the works of the law shall no flesh be justified.*

You are not alone in troubles if you trust Me even in your distress
When you succumb to fear's cold clutch your nights are sleepless
Will you struggle in the dark to breathe, or will you learn the secret
*Learn, Love and Laugh* at failures and hardships, and you progress

I Am not moved by the acceptance of My will in sorrowful resignation
Only seeing you in good humor while trusting Me in every condition
Inspiring confidence, making men stronger by your daring disposition
For My children trapped in sorrow and sin, longing for transformation

To attack fear, speak My Word when the devil's fangs seek your throat
Remember My cry, "It is finished" I died on the Cross, your scapegoat
Death and life are in the tongue; My disciples were terrified in the boat
I spoke to the wind, calmed the waves, and their hearts stayed afloat

It was My Word that dealt with the Tempter when 40 days I had fasted
Fear is not a weakness; it is a temptation to be attacked and defeated
It is a sin to give in or refuse to believe that your salvation is completed
The "Sword of the Spirit" conquers; saved by grace, your Faith is gifted

## July 2

## Only Believe

**Matthew 18:1–3**
*And Jesus called a little child unto him, and set him in the midst of them, And said, Verily I say unto you, Except ye be converted, and become as little children, ye shall not enter into the kingdom of heaven.*

All the obstacles in your journey cannot impede your progress
You'd like to know what lies ahead; it robs Faith of sweetness
Boldly face the future; do not live in dread, trust Me, and witness
Worry not about what is coming, where it leads or try to guess

Know Faith is all you need; you do not have to see, only believe
Many came for cures; I taught according to Faith, you receive
Childlike and humble you must become, nothing up your sleeve
For salvation, wonderworking, and healing, Faith is the one key

Do passing years add the mind of the trusting child to your nature?
Or are you fearful for tomorrow or and controlled by dread and fear?
Only little children are welcome in My Kingdom; My Word is clear
Friendly and loving — helpful, not cynical, to everyone they endear

# July 3

## The Mystery

**Isaiah 55:1–2**

*Ho, everyone that thirsteth, come ye to the waters, and he that hath no money; come ye, buy, and eat; yea, come, buy wine and milk without money and without price. Wherefore do ye spend money for that which is not bread? And your labour for that which satisfieth not?*

Do you realize My feeding of the Thousands was only an illustration?
One day the world will know I Am the Bread of Life for all the nations
Eternal life-giving food for man to eat, scorning death and corruption
It is a mystery understood only by humble hearts in their regeneration

Many do not believe in the Incarnation; how could God be born in a stable?
2,000 years now, and My time on earth remains a mystery to many people
They do not believe I came to earth to save them; they think it is a fable
Uncaring how before time, I planned their salvation eternally irrevocable

Satisfying physical needs, few men hunger and thirst for righteousness

But spiritual life is vital; abiding in Me alone you discover true happiness
It is a journey that takes a lifetime, trusting My workmanship in progress
An expedition into My living Word, undertaken in obedience for success

I hide My mysteries from the wise, admitting only the meek and humble
Let not your hearts be troubled with sin and sorrow; My grace is reliable
Nailed to My Cross, only I could die and rise again; you are not culpable
It is your freedom; no one can take it from you; in Me, you are invincible

## July 4

### Great Friend

**John 15:13**
*Greater love hath no man than this, that a man lay down his life for his friends.*

Transformation begins when you discover you have a Great Friend
Theology is your learning about Me; why you can entirely depend
Holiness is growing steadily in My likeness, in obedience transcend
Perfection is your heavenly Father's call, trusting My grace to mend

Reflect often on I Am; your Great Friend; Creator, Lord, and Savior
Be thrilled and amazed that God is even closer than your neighbor
Alert, ready to help, discerning needs, protecting you in every danger
Faithful companion, loving, untiring, miracle man, your safe harbor

I Am God; I Am your friend no matter what you do or what may befall
Over life's mountains and valleys, I will guide you, taking charge overall

Without saying a word, we are in perfect union, whether day or nightfall
Never will I condemn nor judge what you do; your sins I will not recall

# July 5

## Invincible

**Psalm 28:7**

*The LORD is my strength and my shield; my heart trusted in him, and I Am*
*helped: therefore my heart greatly rejoiceth; and with my song will I praise*
*him.*

Place all your hopes in Me; I Am your Lord; no other could love you more
In the palm of My hand, My eye is on you, alert to bless; I will never ignore
No weapon formed against you can prosper; I Am ahead of you, I go before
My Will stands forever, no matter your defeats, fear not, eternity is in store

A traveler on the high seas trembles as each wave seems to overwhelm
Tossed about any vessel could lose its course, despite plans, or stratagem
With mighty winds and waves, the sea is a frightening, dangerous realm
I Am the Captain of your ship; your salvation secured, I Am at the helm

## July 6

## No More Doubts

**Acts 10:19–20**

*While Peter thought on the vision, the Spirit said unto him, Behold, three men seek thee. Arise therefore, and get thee down, and go with*
*them, doubting nothing: for I have sent them.*

Never believe you cannot achieve or afford what is within My Will
My timing is perfect; your provision comes; wait, sharpen your skill
Stay the course, be diligent in everything at hand; do not stand still
Trusting Me builds your Faith; for all your needs, I consistently fulfill

When you have no doubts about receiving My supply, it is evidence
You know you receive according to Faith; it proves your confidence
Not just as Faith expressed in prayer and praise as a mere observance
But a conviction that conquers all doubts as they arise with a violence

# July 7

## Full Rein of Your Heart

**Romans 8:28**
*And we know that all things work together for good to them that love*
*God, to them who are the called according to his purpose.*

You have a lifework to do, for I designed you to share a message
The hardships you faced in Peace and Joy, show Me your courage
One day you will understand the reason was to build you, not damage
As a witness to tell of your Savior who sets men free from bondage

Success that the world chases after will bring you little satisfaction
Your yearnings, both material and spiritual; I will balance and action
Let Me have full rein within your heart, and you will live without tension
Believe I will supply all things for your journey and trust My provision

## July 8

## Where I Go

**Ruth 1:16**

*And Ruth said, intreat me not to leave thee, or to return from following*
*after thee: for whither thou goest, I will go; and where thou lodgest, I will lodge: thy people shall be my people, and thy God my God.*

Without Me, no matter what you accomplish, you will feel hollow
Trust in My guidance, obey all My instructions as I lead and follow
I may point to new places; but where I go, there is nothing shallow
Your desires must accord with My Will; in one mind, My work fellow

# July 9

## Do Not Doubt

**Hebrews 10:39**

*But we are not of them who draw back unto perdition; but of them that believe to the saving of the soul.*

Creator and Savior, people doubt I Am; for all it is no sin to question
To those skeptical about My Love, it is okay; disbelief is anyone's option
I Am Your Guardian, have no qualms or ignorance about My position
For constant fear and worry in your life indicates little transformation

Life is a spiritual swamp without Me at the helm, in every circumstance
How can you realize I Am your Lord and Savior if you keep a distance?
You cannot settle for knowing Me with no depth or Faith in My Presence
Be one with the Father, Son, and Holy Spirit, and be complete in essence

## July 10

## Guarded

**Job 1:10**

*Hast not thou made an hedge about him, and about his house, and about*
*all that he hath on every side? thou hast blessed the work of his hands,*
*and his substance is increased in the land.*

You may not know it, but I protect you in ways unknown and invisible
To keep you from harm in situations you get into that need a miracle
Nothing happens to you without My permission if you stay in My Will
Every day of your life covered by My guardianship in the supernatural

# July 11

## In My Keeping

**Psalm 91:1–2**

*He that dwelleth in the secret place of the most High shall abide under*
*the shadow of the Almighty. I will say of the LORD, He is my refuge and*
*my fortress: my God; in him will I trust.*

How can you forget that you are the children of the Creator and King
I Am the Owner; I have the deed stamped and sealed in My keeping
My heavenly hosts surround you; your every move they keep tracking
Night and day defend you from enemies you cannot see while walking

## July 12

## Formidable Savior

**Galatians 5:1**

*Stand fast therefore in the liberty wherewith Christ hath made us free, and be not entangled again with the yoke of bondage.*

Believe in your deliverance and be sure of your eternal salvation
No one can snatch you from My hand; formidable My protection
A drowning man rescued is not taken to a more dangerous location
You are home and dry on solid ground; live boldly, reject tension

I broke the chains of slavery in Egypt, for I Am your eternal Savior
You are safe and secure in the palm of My hand, clad in My armor
Hunted no more in the valley of death, no evil can harm you or devour
You may have many battle scars; of My Love, make them a reminder

I'd gladly remove all hardships, but trial by fire gives you an advantage
Trust and obey; know I Am in control; no power on earth can sabotage
On the Cross, when I cried, "It is finished," I also meant your bondage
In a fallen world of death, tell men of your Savior's life-saving message

## July 13

### More Power

**Psalm 34:4**
*I sought the LORD, and he heard me, and delivered me from all my fears.*

Where the Spirit of the Lord is, there is authentic freedom
That is true Faith, not religion; it is My Power and Wisdom
A life of obedience will bring you fulfillment, not boredom
I deny things you yearn, for greater heights in My Kingdom

The more Power you receive, the more Freedom you obtain
Constantly ask, Lord, what do you want me to do; be certain
Let the Spirit live in you, and get clear direction as I explain
I gave My Life to set you free; let no doubts of My Will remain

Faith in Me should keep your heart utterly free from fear
No matter where you are or what happens, know I am near
You, are My dearest thought; there is nothing I do not hear
Do you trust Me like a child or believe My Will is unclear?

# July 14

## True Success

**Joshua 1:8**
*This book of the law shall not depart out of thy mouth; but thou shalt meditate therein day and night, that thou mayest observe to do according to all that is written therein: for then thou shalt make thy way prosperous, and then thou shalt have good success.*

Have no doubts; go forward unafraid and sure of My guidance
Remember how the Israelite's crossed the Red Sea in confidence
You, too, are protected; proceed without delay in My Presence
It is your new phase of progress as you overcome the resistance

Age does not matter in eternal life, so that is not a disadvantage
Let Joy and gratitude mark your journey at every stage of passage
You have learned to overcome challenges, free of every bondage
Now conquer in My Love, ready to witness and share My message

# July 15

## Your Fortress

**Psalm 91:9–10**
*Because thou hast made the LORD, which is my refuge, even the most High, thy habitation; There shall no evil befall thee, neither shall any plague come nigh thy dwelling.*

To climb the spiritual ladder, I have given clear lessons in scripture
First, consider, would I plant your feet on broken rungs you fear?
All the steps may not be visible; I expect you to trust I do not injure
My martyrs did not have that assurance, only knew eternity was secure

Remember how they went singing on their way, alone and friendless
Setting aside their doubts, they struggled but trusting, not hopeless
Joy and confidence must symbolize your journey, too, not distress
For the secret place of the Most High you dwell in, is your fortress

## July 16

## My Secret Place

**Psalm 25:14**
*The secret of the LORD is with them that fear him; and he will show them his covenant.*

Divine Power empowers you to trust and dwell in My Love
Your childlike Faith and trusting laughter come from above
Safety is in My secret place; you fly on the wings of a Dove
There in My strong tower you abide where nobody can shove

# July 17

## I Will Transform

**Mark 4:39**
*And he arose, and rebuked the wind, and said unto the sea,*
*Peace, be still. And the wind ceased, and there was a great calm.*

Rejoice that you have much to learn; from you, I will not conceal
I do not withdraw My Presence when more of My Truth I reveal
The storms of life will pass like the wind in My disciple's ordeal
I will always be there to help you whenever you make an appeal

My Kingdom lessons you learn when at peace or during a storm
But there will come relief to comfort you and restore your calm
You will rest in My Presence, under My Shield, and I will transform
Reborn in Me, to the old pattern of the world, you will not conform

## July 18

## Sanctification

**Matthew 5:8**
*Blessed are the pure in heart, for they shall see our God.*

You love Me and know My name; I will free you and set you on high
Shun the broad way that leads to perdition; seek My Purity to fortify
Disregard the world's seduction; your fleshly passions will not satisfy
I transform your temptations in My sanctification, your soul to qualify

## July 19

## Greatest Miracle

**Psalm 86:10**

*For thou art great, and doest wondrous things: thou art God alone.*

Follow Me, and a remarkable life unfolds for you in security
Your Guide and Friend, always beside you; joy in My reality
My children see miracles every day by discerning spiritually
Others believe it is contrary to nature, and view things sensually

The natural man is an enemy of God; saved only by a new birth
A holy conversion setting you free; the greatest miracle on earth
By Grace, you experience that phenomenon and learn your worth
Set apart in My Kingdom; in Faith, humility, and justice, go forth

Remember, My child; it is not a journey of quick or easy transformation
Testing and training in the crucible; impossible without My intervention
Battling your sins and failures can take many years until your integration
In My Spiritual Power, you conquer self, clear evidence of your condition

## July 20

## Outcome My Responsibility

**John 10:4–5**

*And when he putteth forth his own sheep, he goeth before them, and*
*the sheep follow him: for they know his voice. And a stranger will they*
*not follow, but will flee from him: for they know not the voice of strangers.*

Results are not your concern; the outcome is My responsibility
My directions are perfect; every rule designed mathematically
You will see the benefits when you employ My Word, obediently
Alert for My teachings and following divine guidance instantly

I will guide you through your fear and doubt as we walk together
Lay aside all earthly goals outside My Will, no matter how clever
When faced with two paths to choose, all you have to do is inquire
Simple trust: but the world knows not, your Faith rests in My Power

# July 21

## Praise Power

**2 Samuel 22:4**
*I will call on the Lord, who is worthy to be praised: so shall I be saved from mine enemies.*

In a world of myth and delusion, praise power beats sacrifice
Lifting your voice in heartfelt praise; always your joyful choice
Through the mud and grime or blood, sweat and tears, rejoice
Follow My lead in flood or fire, and you will delight in My service

Sing a million hallelujahs, and let My praises ring every moment
Try it when trouble comes; thank Me through it all, be constant
I delivered David from the hand of his enemies; it was no accident
Praise can move mountains; test My Word; you must experiment

## July 22

## Comforts Can Confuse

**1 Peter 3:15**

*But sanctify the Lord God in your hearts: and be ready always to give*
*an answer to every man that asketh you a reason of the hope that is in*
*you with meekness and fear.*

The blind, the lame, and lepers I healed; the poor heard the Gospel
My Father and I call you to do far greater work based on My model
Can I raise the dead, you ask, there are other tasks also supernatural
By My Holy Spirit, help save the lost; My Great Commission fulfill

Be a witness of My Grace and forgiveness, sharing the Good News
Often My children forget their purpose in life; comforts can confuse
You are in the world but not to be of the world; My Love, do not abuse
For so many lost souls, the laborers are so few; your Call do not refuse

## July 23

### Whatever Happens

**Philippians 4:7**
*And the peace of God, which passeth all understanding, shall keep your hearts and minds through Christ Jesus.*

Seek My Peace; it passes all understanding; none can shake or disrupt
But fear and despair can overcome when you give in; they interrupt
And an overwhelming world of worry and anxiety, you then construct
Cease all activity, and I will restore My calm before you go bankrupt

There is some training, you need to know My Peace with confidence
I allow trials and hardships; they help you mature, make a difference
While you abide in the shadow of the Most High God, in His Presence
That He cares for sparrows and the lilies of the field is clear evidence

Fear not, I urge you every day; I walk with you, constantly beside
Only do not forget I control everything; whatever happens, I decide

If there is a storm brewing or a tempest forecast, in Me, run and hide
I will see you through all life's whirlwinds as your Savior and guide

## July 24

## Complete Confidence

**Psalm 121:5–8**

*The LORD is thy keeper: the LORD is thy shade upon thy right hand.*
*The sun shall not smite thee by day, nor the moon by night. The LORD*
*shall preserve thee from all evil: he shall preserve thy soul. The LORD*
*shall preserve thy going out and thy coming in from this time forth, and*
*even for evermore.*

I Am the Way, the Truth and the Life, the answer to every question
Look for nothing more; no one else can save; there is no other option
They will attempt, but no enemy can harm you when in My protection
In My Presence, live and move and have your being, the only condition

In Me alone are the secrets of Power, Peace, Purity, and all significance
Anchored firmly, release all your burdens to Me with complete confidence
Discern My Will, gain enough strength for the day and obtain My guidance
Then go forth to conquer whatever comes your way with no disturbance

## July 25

## No Separation

**Ephesians 1:7**
*In whom we have redemption through his blood, the forgiveness of sins, according to the riches of his grace.*

I Am Creator, Lord, and Savior. Your life's eternal custodian
Forget your past; for the present and future, I Am your guardian
Trust Me with your plans, heed My call and serve in obedience
You are in the palm of My hands; God-guided in your diligence

Yours is the miracle of divine security, the blessings of salvation
There is nothing more incredible than new birth—your recreation
Laugh at evil when it hounds you; it cannot cause our separation
I redeemed you forever; none can snatch you in My Resurrection

# July 26

## Evidence of Love

**Matthew 5:43–48**

*But I say unto you, Love your enemies, bless them that curse you, do good to them that hate you, and pray for them which despitefully use you, and persecute you.*

Consider not the hurts of the past; forgive all who were malevolent
Life is short; fill it with My Love and laughter; it's the best investment
You may not share the same point of view but treat all as equivalent
Let others do what they do; remember it is Me whom you represent

Break down barriers, do not build walls because of your vain ambition
I made you all in My image to share My Love and mercy in true union
Show the world you are My disciples, with evidence of transformation
Obey My new commandment to love as I have loved in all your action

## July 27

## My Consolation

**Ephesians 1:3–4**
*Blessed be the God and Father of our Lord Jesus Christ, who hath blessed us with all spiritual blessings in heavenly places in Christ: According as he hath chosen us in him before the foundation of the world, that we should be holy and without blame before him in love.*

You will grasp the depth of My Love when you understand
The comfort I feel walking beside you, holding your hand
I don't need to be near to protect you, do not misunderstand
But your love and trust in Me bring Me solace; it is so grand

My children, it is not one-sided, for you can move My heart
Don't you find joy, treasure those you love and hate to part?
That is how it is with Me; for I knew you from the very start
Our relationship began before creation; nothing can thwart

## July 28

### None Can Overpower

**Psalm 3:3–5**
*But thou, O Lord, art a shield for me; my glory, and the lifter up of mine head.*

Between all the disrespect and indignity of the world, I Am your shield
Remember that constantly until nothing has power to disturb or wield
Then the victory is yours, a state of marvelous inward peace is sealed
Knowing I Am the lifter of your head, My glory tasted once, never yield

My Word is subtle; you often wonder why I allow you to make mistakes
Especially at times when you try hard to do My Will, knowing the stakes
Hopes fade away when your cherished plans abruptly slam the brakes
Because some lessons in life's story you learn only after several retakes

By and by, the mists start to lift, when the depths of My Word you plumb
And you find favor and understanding with God and man, and then some

Conquering the flaws in your nature that have dominated you one by one
My promises not for those who face no hurdles but for all who overcome

## July 29

### My Delight

**Ephesians 1:18**

*The eyes of your understanding being enlightened; that ye may know*
*what is the hope of his calling, and what the riches of the glory of his*
*inheritance in the saints.*

Suffering is not the only route into My Kingdom; count every blessing
The symphony of life in Spring, gentle breezes, the warm sun shining
Raindrops on pink petals, colors of the rainbow, red sunsets flaming
Some of the joys in creation for My children I include in My training

But to help you know that suffering is no option in your life's journeys
There is great thunder and lightning, vast mountains, and deep valleys
Designed for your delight, to mark the achievements of your odysseys
As you reminisce by the fireside, gladly home from arduous journeys

But leave all those trials in My hand; trust Me in darkness and sunlight
I know what you can bear and restrict your temptations for you to fight

My Kingdom is in you, not in the world I have overcome for your right
To your eternal inheritance nobody can take away or claim, My delight

# July 30

## Battle Tested

**John 20:29**

*Jesus saith unto him, Thomas, because thou hast seen me, thou hast*
*believed: blessed are they that have not seen, and yet have believed.*

I Am the Ancient of Days; learn of Me from My people who struggled
My promise of a nation, seed and his heir, patriarch Abraham, believed
Esther could have lost her life but observe how valiantly she modeled
David slayed Goliath; Daniel tamed lions; in Faith, many marveled

Many down the ages have not seen yet believed, often in great danger
The ultimate test may not be your Calling, but still, as My messenger
You must learn how to overcome when in life you face a cliffhanger
For in heaven, you will be a battle-tested veteran, not mere passenger

## July 31

## Gratitude

**1 Thessalonians 5:18**
*In every thing give thanks: for this is the will of God in Christ Jesus concerning you.*

Offer up to Me the loving gift of a courageous and grateful heart
It is the ability to see reasons to praise Me that will set you apart
Life's challenges should engage you in thankfulness from the start
Tender a consecration of praise to Me, with sweet incense impart

In varied unusual ways, taste My showers of blessings as they flow
Practice a benediction diligently every day, and soon you will know
You can be thankful for everything, for, in your gratitude, you show
Trust in Me no matter what happens, and your love for Me will grow

# August

## August 1

### Eternal Oneness In Me

**2 Corinthians 5:17**
*Therefore if any man be in Christ, he is a new creature: old things are passed away; behold, all things are become new.*

I gave up My Life for you; I will never leave nor forsake you
No bond on earth is like ours; for My own, I forever pursue
I Am your Maker, Redeemer and Friend, taste, see, I Am true
Oneness in Me is the treasure that makes your life brand new

## August 2

## Fertile Ground

**Matthew 13:8**

*But other fell into good ground, and brought forth fruit, some an hundredfold, some sixty fold, some thirty fold.*

Remember My parable of the seed with four distinct types of soil
Only one proved fruitful with abundant produce, for it was fertile
I Am the Sower; I love to bestow choice blessings on your life's toil
But hearts riddled with stones, thorns, are without depth, in turmoil

Man's free choice enables different responses to My life-giving feed
You must be tillable enough for Me to plant just a tiny mustard seed
Preparing the soil is your responsibility, for My planting is guaranteed
Together we reap the harvest, sharing joy in the results as we succeed

Prayer is the best soil fertilizer; keep trusting Me you will pull through
Accept your hardships as paths to Peace, never forget I Am with you

Seek to be reasonably happy on earth, but home is far beyond the blue
Until then, live in the perfection of every single moment till I greet you

## August 3

## Let Me Streamline

**1 Timothy 6:9**

*But they that will be rich fall into temptation and a snare, and into many foolish and hurtful lusts, which drown men in destruction and perdition.*

When I hear the cry of My children demanding all of Me, what a thrill
Wanting Me in every action, thought, word and moment, I'd love to fill
The greatest gift I cherish is your time and trust, surrendering your will
Childlike love, steadfast and true, make me hasten your dreams to fulfill

But giving Me your all is no easy lesson, even if your longing is genuine
Your pet projects, dreams to go here and there, do this and that, routine
Giving Me the moments means giving up your goals, some joys decline
You can only achieve this if you keep your eyes fixed; let Me streamline

Not all can embark on this journey; only a few come through this initiation
Those hearts attuned to the cries of souls desperate for eternal Salvation

Honoring the plea of their Savior seeking to fulfill His Great Commission
Willing laborers in His vineyard cheerfully forsaking their earthly ambition

## August 4

## You Live in Eternity

**Psalm 16:11**

*Thou wilt shew me the path of life: in thy presence is fulness of joy; at thy right hand there are pleasures for evermore.*

To know Me is eternal life; a glorious journey begins to your inheritance
A seamless sojourn as wonders unfold, life is complete in My Presence
Spirit, mind, and body cleansed, healed, restored, and renewed in essence
And My miracle-working Power flowing out of you to all in convergence

Abide in Me constantly, fully aware of My company with total conviction
Do not be driven to work ceaselessly; rest in Me, achieve without tension
Each moment you spend with Me, the more your joy grows in communion
You live in eternity, in the Power of My Spirit; nothing counts but our union

What should matter now is what will last forever; earthly things they all decay
Keep your eyes fixed on things above, not on the things that surely fade away

Life is a symphony echoing My Words; I Am the Life, the Truth, and the Way
Everlasting happiness and security are yours now; go share My Love every day

## August 5

## Never Forsaken

**Hebrews 10:37**

*For yet a little while, and he that shall come will come, and will not tarry.*

Does a loved one have to beg for help when in overwhelming need?
Wouldn't you come alongside them even before they cry and plead?
A father or mother may forsake you, but My provision is guaranteed
When it seems you can't, in Me, you can; My Love never fails to lead

Mine is the Love that brooks no tortured pleading from My children
I send My Word to deliver you from harm and heal the heartbroken
In your time of need, I do not tarry, nor do I place a heavy burden
Every moment I see everything you do, for never are you forsaken

## August 6

## Enter My Rest

**Hebrews 4:9–11**
*There remaineth therefore a rest to the people of God. For he that is entered*
*Into his rest, he also hath ceased from his own works, as God did from his.*
*Let us labour therefore to enter into that rest, lest any man fall after the same*
*example of unbelief.*

While on earth, I needed My time of rest and communion with My Father
Surely you, too, need to break away from stress and life's daily clamor
I have made a rest for you to cease work and seek My Presence to enter
You need refilling in the Holy Spirit; He will guide you into Truth and Power

From that place of healing, go forth to bless others and share My grace
Tell people they are strong in their weaknesses if My Word they embrace
For I give them rest when things go wrong, and their sins I will not trace
All those seeking God's mercy and favor will receive Faith and My solace

## August 7

## Let Me Rescue

**Psalm 91:14–15**

*Because he hath set his love upon me, therefore will I deliver him: I will set him on high, because he hath known my name. He shall call upon me, and I will answer him: I will be with him in trouble; I will*
*deliver him, and honour him.*

Man's disbelief, dread and despair make a mockery of My Love
My faithfulness is indisputable; still, unbelief demands I prove
Is there greater proof than God coming down to die from above?
Why do you not believe? Why do you still worry, push and shove?

When you fall into sin, I do not hide My face; I never abandon you
You may feel confused, fear and doubt rush in when you lose virtue
It is time for you to pray; delve deep into My Word and let Me rescue
When you humbly trust in My Mercy and Grace, believe they are true

## August 8

## Law of Supply

**Matthew 6:31–32**

*Therefore take no thought, saying, What shall we eat? or, What shall*
*we drink? or, Wherewithal shall we be clothed? For after all these*
*things do the Gentiles seek: for your heavenly Father knoweth that*
*ye have need of all these things.*

I Am your reliable supply, depend on no other, live in My Spirit of trust
Do not hoard My blessings, share My Love with others, do not be unjust
The more you keep, the less you obtain, for My law of supply will adjust
Holding back indicates a lack of Faith and fear of the future; it is mistrust

Trust Me to save you from the sea of poverty; it frightens you; I Am aware
If your Faith is genuine, demonstrate it, and be cheerfully willing to share
Clinging to your meagre resources to save yourself shows you do not care
Depend on Me, whatever the circumstances fear not; I will always be there

I will fill your bucket if you empty it in trust; it is a difficult lesson to learn
But unless you do, you will depend on your riches, not on Me, as you earn

A drowning man trying to save himself causes his deliverer
more concern
Only when rendered helpless, can he be saved; the rescuer's
love discern

## August 9

## Transform Tension

**1 Timothy 5:18**

*For the scripture saith, Thou shalt not muzzle the ox that treadeth out the corn. And, The labourer is worthy of his reward.*

I Am ever present, ever near, come to Me and learn of My ways
They are sure they are safe; when you abide in Me, I will amaze
You have nothing to fear, for I will never leave you all your days
Trust Me every moment, and in all your troubles, learn to praise

Be faithful in My vineyard, working side by side with Me in union
Labor and rest combine in My Kingdom; there is no competition
You bear much fruit by Faith and effort with ample compensation
Learning to prioritize living in My Presence transforms all tension

## August 10

## Mission Completed

**Psalm 59:16**
*But I will sing of thy power; yea, I will sing aloud of thy mercy in the morning: for thou hast been my defence and refuge in the day of my trouble.*

You cannot keep from straying unless you abide in Me constantly
It is the only way to overcome temptation and avoid snares deftly
Nothing can separate us; I Am the Light, showing your path clearly
If you follow My direction, you will stay on track beside Me, surely

My Peace, I have promised, not a life of ease, comfort, and pleasure
In the world, you have tribulation, but it is not a sign of your failure
I have overcome the world, cheerfully see adversity as an adventure
Under My guidance, every challenge taken is a memory to treasure

I was spat upon, scourged, misunderstood, forsaken, and crucified
Victoriously I cried, "It is finished," My mission completed, ratified

My overcoming Power will sustain you, too, when you are terrified
Failure, distress, or danger cannot conquer My children sanctified

## August 11

## In My Fortress

**Psalm 18:2**
*The LORD is my rock, and my fortress, and my deliverer; my God, my strength, in whom I will trust; my buckler, and the horn of my salvation, and my high tower.*

I Am the Light of the world; no shadows hide in My brightness
You are My precious child; fear not, I will dispel your darkness
Turn disquiet to quiet, turmoil to tranquil, problems to progress
Have complete Faith in Me; never lose hope; safe in My fortress

My Father made a splendid, orderly world from nothing, a void
Flinging the stars into space, He set the seasons that you enjoy
For you, His magnificent creation, all His resources they deploy
Live in Me; My Father and I are one; your peacefulness, Our joy

Doesn't it follow naturally that all your affairs are mine to order?
Whatever task you undertake, your difficulties I will shoulder
If you abide in My Will, whatever happens, you will not go under
Stay faithful to My Word; chaos is in climbing the world's ladder

## August 12

## Change Your World

**Isaiah 61:1**

*The Spirit of the Lord God is upon me; because the Lord hath anointed*
*me to preach good tidings unto the meek; he hath sent me to bind up the*
*brokenhearted, to proclaim liberty to the captives, and the opening of*
*the prison to them that are bound.*

Keep this in mind; I answer every prayer in My time, none do I ignore
But do not use prayer only for your needs for everything you implore
Be burdened to pray for the wrongs you see that may need Me more
For problems in your nation, politicians, its laws, include your arch foe

Since every prayer gets answered; your obligation to pray is compelling
If you persist, lives will change, new laws made, and evil sent packing
Make your humble prayer room the power source for the world, changing
You may never see your mighty work, but I will; Satan dreads My renewing

I call you to live large; a life of service is something you should treasure

Be My hands of compassion to save My people, your greatest adventure
You will make a difference in this world, and your success will last forever
Triumphant is the life that takes the good news of My Salvation wherever

## August 13

## Blameless

**Romans 8:1–3**

*There is therefore now no condemnation to them which are in Christ Jesus,*
*who walk not after the flesh, but after the Spirit. For the law of the Spirit of*
*life in Christ Jesus hath made me free from the law of sin and death. For*
*what the law could not do, in that it was weak through the flesh, God sending*
*his own Son in the likeness of sinful flesh, and for sin, condemned sin in the*
*flesh.*

I Am your helpmate leading you into My Light out of your darkness
Filling you with the Holy Spirit, to receive My Power, lose weakness
Saving you from Sin to Salvation; rescuing from danger, poverty, stress
Transforming your life with My Love by assuring perfect forgiveness

"Be ye perfect even as your Father in Heaven is perfect," I demand
Have you considered why I gave you such an impossible command?
In My death and Resurrection, your Redemption, I thoroughly planned

When I cried, "it is finished," I made you blameless; none can reprimand

But if you say you have no sin, you deceive yourself; that is not the truth
You make Me a liar with such a claim, for you sin till old age from youth
Review your failings in life with God and man, acknowledge your untruth
I have forgiven your sins, but follow Me in every situation, do not be uncouth

## August 14

## My Priceless Gift

**Ephesians 1:3–4**

*Blessed be the God and Father of our Lord Jesus Christ, who hath blessed us*
*with all spiritual blessings in heavenly places in Christ: According as he hath*
*chosen us in him before the foundation of the world, that we should be holy*
*and without blame before him in love.*

Your uncommon riches are spiritual, mental, physical, joy and power
So precious an abundant life, yet many believe My gift does not matter
The priceless, most incomparable gift of Heaven has very few takers!
Free for all, but rejected by proud men and women scorning the Maker

I Am the Way, the Truth, the Life; reject not My Father's gift to you
His Mercy and Grace sets you free from sin; eternal life is in view
Water from the fountain of life, a never to thirst again heavenly brew
Chosen in Him before the world began, to be holy, for He foreknew

## August 15

## I Stand Beside

**Psalm 25:8–9**

*Good and upright is the LORD: therefore will he teach sinners in the way. The meek will he guide in judgment: and the meek will he teach his way.*

I do not punish you for sins, Past, Present or Future, have no fear
But good and evil have consequences; you know that it is clear
Violating spiritual or physical laws using free will; I do not interfere
But there are hard lessons to learn, and they can be quite severe

Nonetheless, through it all, I stand beside you though you disobey
Waiting for you to bounce back and confess your sins without delay
If you listened when your conscience spoke up, you would not betray
Unconfessed sin separates us, leaves you unguarded, stalked as prey

I long for you to know My Calling for your life, designed just for you
It will bring you such joy and passion in doing what I meant you to do
My children would know Me sooner if I Am served by those who knew
Fishers of men, obeying My Word in heart, soul, and mind, true-blue

## August 16

## Never Alone

**Deuteronomy 31:6**

*Be strong and courageous. Do not be afraid or terrified because of them,*
*for the LORD your God goes with you; he will never leave you nor forsake*
*you.*

Do not be driven; rest in Me often for eternal life you have entered
There is no need to work under stress; your every hair I've numbered
Worry no more, eternity flows through your veins; your life is ordered
I equip you with gifts to carry out My Calling, and I keep you inspired

I know you cannot quite make it through the day struggling on your own
You need My love to guide you; I Am your Savior; I will never abandon
I Am always listening to your troubles, and I will not let you breakdown
Life is a journey of ups and downs but remember that you are not alone

## August 17

## Enjoy My Creation

**Psalm 8:3–4**

*When I consider thy heavens, the work of thy fingers, the moon and the stars, which thou hast ordained; What is man, that thou art mindful of him? and the son of man, that thou visitest him?*

Holiday in My sunshine, in the fresh air; stay connected
The great outdoors, the sun's warmth, medicines I created
Enjoy My creation; I Am with you; you are never isolated
Have Trust and Faith, My prescription for a life dedicated

Nature is the cathedral of My Father's prolific imagination
He knew mind, soul, and body needed refreshing variation
His dew from Heaven sparkles like diamonds in perception
And nature nurses faint souls fatigued, seeking recreation

## August 18

## Loving Acceptance

**Psalm 112:7**
*He shall not be afraid of evil tidings: his heart is fixed, trusting in the LORD.*

Distance does not separate us; earth's miles do not matter
What tries to separate us is falsehood, and when fears enter
Your training is rigorous; your work for Me nothing can hinder
If you seek Me, you shall find, but your will can you surrender?

It is not the searching as much as yielding to Me in everything
Consciously submitting to Me unconditionally, not withholding
In all matters, big or small, you allow Me to guide you, trusting
Opposing every wrong with truth, unshorn, unshod, and believing

What a different companion is one always joyful in My Presence
Cheerfully accepting My direction, never doubting My guidance
And another who is rebellious, must be forced, fakes acceptance
Does not want to be alone, and hates going My Way, is a nuisance

It is not the road, My child, but your loving acceptance is important
You can use your God-given free will; you are not to be a sycophant
I know what lies ahead; you need My guidance; life can be turbulent
In Me alone can all your needs be met, but your attitude is significant

## August 19

## Scions in Training

**Galatians 4:7**

*Wherefore thou art no more a servant, but a son; and if a son, then an*
*heir of God through Christ.*

Worship Me in Spirit and Truth; innate in man is the adoration of God
Be aware that I Am human and divine, or your understanding is flawed
I became a mortal to raise you to My Divinity; the heavenly host is awed
By God's eternal intent for man's blessed end and His salvation method

Earth offered a consecrated human temple, Mary's womb, for My Divinity
Divine Power, Love and Peace empower all My children who believe in Me
Understand who you are, heirs of almighty God, preserve a spirit of humility
Majesty, power, and beauty await a heavenly life of such infinite nobility

When it comes to My giving, that is limitless; it is only your accepting
Called to wonders you cannot imagine, view them in prayer, believing

To attain them, rise in My Love and Power, and be filled with a longing
Strive to be perfect in Faith; you are scions of God and Christ in training

## August 20

## Wins, Losses and Draws

**Romans 6:14**

*For sin shall not have dominion over you: for ye are not under the law, but under grace.*

I had to shield Peter from hating himself after his bitter betrayal
He almost lost his will to live; I showed him My Love is radical
Scorned neither by My Father nor Me, his contempt was personal
Remember, whatever you may do, your failures are never terminal

My children, you often denounce yourselves for one or many failures
Friends may resent, and enemies sneer, and often self-hatred appears
I shield you not from My Father's anger; He is all Love; it is your fears
Nor do you receive My condemnation, for in Me your sin disappears

You mean to be steadfast, loyal to Me, but in your flesh is no good thing
Only in My shield of Love can you struggle and conquer in life's setting
But when you fail, guilt and regret are inevitable; you are still in training
A beautiful butterfly emerges from the chrysalis, proof of My transforming

Do not dwell even for a moment on your past sins or any of your flaws
You are now under My Grace, subject no more to Old Testament laws
In life's race, you stumble as you press on, with wins, losses and draws
You get a fresh start every day; your freedom inevitably a life of seesaws

I sent My disciples out, two by two, with no bag or coats, and no money
My instructions they were to obey boldly, depending on Me completely
You, too, must get rid of all extra baggage as you travel in life's journey
Discarding any sense of failure, with a light heart in My Love's security

## August 21

### Covenant Not Contract

**Leviticus 26:44**
*And yet for all that, when they be in the land of their enemies, I will not*
*cast them away, neither will I abhor them, to destroy them utterly, and*
*to break my covenant with them: for I [am] the LORD their God.*

Behold, I make all things new; it is the worldly spirit that cannot soar
My blessings cut your ties to the earth, poverty and worry you abhor
The joy of My freedom lifts you into the realm of gratitude as I restore
Broken wings grow again, life revels in beauty, strength more and more

Give Me your burdens to carry; confess your sins and let nothing distract
My promise of renewal I fulfill; delight in your Power to make an impact
"All ye that labor and are heavy laden, I will give rest." My Word is exact
Confess your sins, you are prone; our covenant is much more than a contract

## August 22

## Beautiful Memories

**Ecclesiastes 7:14**

*In the day of prosperity be joyful, but in the day of adversity consider:*
*God also hath set the one over against the other, to the end that man*
*should find nothing after him.*

Do you want My world redeemed and help to bring its transformation?
If you care, your suffering can save others and lead to their salvation
But there is training required before you can engage in such mediation
Offer up trials and troubles, cherish hardships for one soul's conversion

Embracing hardships can also have prayers for special needs answered
Learn from My suffering on earth; I did not desire comforts; I labored
Choose to save others, sing when afflictions arise, do not be bewildered
Each day of adversity then becomes a beautiful memory to be treasured

## August 23

## Don't Be Passive

**Isaiah 40:4**
*Every valley shall be exalted, and every mountain and hill shall be made low: and the crooked shall be made straight, and the rough places plain.*

Ignore the day's hassles and trials; stay focused on life's direction
Mountain climbing is weary if every obstruction causes you tension
A great outdoor adventure, and you have an uninspiring disposition
See every step of the ascent as taking you to your eternal ambition

Every mountain you come across in your journey of life, you wonder
It seems impossible to climb that high; you start to worry and ponder
You conclude it's beyond what you can achieve, give up and stay under
How can I ever use you in My vineyard if you keep hiding in a corner?

Do not be immovable and stay where you are; that is a life unproductive
Move into what your heavenly Father has for you, with a keen initiative
Let nothing hold you back from going deeper into Faith; do not be passive

Challenges are to keep you relying on Me alone to reach your objective

I want you to step out in complete trust and overcome every mountain
Rise to conquer your hindrances, and you will grow if you don't complain
Do not cower in fear if you want to know what God wants you to obtain
As hard as it seems, My glory awaits you, so believe in Me, your Captain

## August 24

## Sublime Heights

**Psalm 17:8–9**

*Keep me as the apple of the eye, hide me under the shadow of thy wings,*
*From the wicked that oppress me, from my deadly enemies, who compass*
*me about.*

I redeemed you; trust Me implicitly; I protect you as the apple of My eye
David knew that is how I saw My people Israel and that's how you qualify
I Am the God who sees you; all things are possible; I will never dissatisfy
You are My precious inheritance; I keep in sight; for you, I ever draw nigh

You are the center of My attention; when you fall into sin, do not despair
I will lift you out of the pit to sublime heights; you are My treasured heir
Know that even if you disobey like the Israelites, My plans will not alter
Confess before Me humbly; I Am your Deliverer, waiting for your prayer

## August 25

## Retain My Guidance

**Psalm 37:23–24**

*The steps of a good man are ordered by the LORD: and he delighteth in his way. Though he fall, he shall not be utterly cast down: for the LORD upholdeth him with his hand.*

Seek Me with all your heart, and you will never pursue Me in vain
Nobody ever sought My help to no end; call on Me; you will obtain
My Spirit responds to your every sigh to restore and refresh again
Sometimes you can be fatigued when My guidance you do not retain

Rest from work when there is too much physical or mental weariness
Or you will lose out on many beautiful situations that bring happiness
I have said My Way is the narrow way, but it is one I abundantly bless
It is wide enough for Me to walk beside you to ensure your progress

## August 26

## Trials Train

**John 3:3**

*Jesus answered and said unto him, Verily, verily, I say unto thee, Except*
*a man be born again, he cannot see the kingdom of God.*

Nothing can overpower you; trials and troubles are only for training
There to implement My Will, which is yours too, in My safekeeping
Understand this clearly; you are invincible, for you have My backing
Rebirth is a brand-new start, your key to My Kingdom that is waiting

You are born again, though still prone to sin, you are saved and accepted
I took your blame; there is no condemnation; it is simple, not complicated
Trust and be confident; know My Presence will never get disconnected
My Grace is sufficient; forget wrong choices made, for you are liberated

## August 27

## Reckless for You

**Samuel 17:45**

*Then David said to the Philistine, "You come to me with a sword, with a spear, and with a javelin. But I come to you in the name of the Lord of hosts, the God of the armies of Israel, whom you have defied."*

Quiet and confident, know you are safe; My Kingdom is a fortress
Faithfully I lead you through danger and distress when hopeless
Without delay, place your life into My hands and all your business
I Am Jehovah Tsaba; when it comes to your safety, I Am reckless

Any discord and disarray, I will transform into order and harmony
Your Great Physician, potent is My cure, minimizing pain tenderly
I long for your trust; everything you go through, I watch carefully
No matter what you face in life, call on Me; I wait for you eagerly

# August 28

## Heaven's Law

**Matthew 22:37–40**

*Jesus said unto him, Thou shalt love the Lord thy God with all thy heart,*
*and with all thy soul, and with all thy mind. This is the first and great*
*commandment. And the second is like unto it, Thou shalt love thy neighbour*
*as thyself. On these two commandments hang all the law and the prophets.*

Live to serve others; it is My law in Heaven, one that the angels obey
Continuous service is what I expect from all who love Me and pray
Whether at rest or busy at work, in every action, even when you play
In My Love, let nothing impede your ministry to people gone astray

## August 29

## Breathe My Name

**Philippians 2:9–11**

*Wherefore God also hath highly exalted him, and given him a name*
*which is above every name: That at the name of Jesus every knee should*
*bow, of things in heaven, and things in earth, and things under the earth;*
*And that every tongue should confess that Jesus Christ is Lord, to the*
*glory of God the Father.*

Jesus. Whisper My Name often. Like a child, put your hand in mine
Hold firm, I can feel your grasp, and I respond with My grip divine
To reassure you of My Presence and to banish fear when you pine
I Am your Savior and Shepherd, My Love for you can never decline

## August 30

## They Are Preferred

**Acts 20:35**

*I have shewed you all things, how that so labouring ye ought to support the weak, and to remember the words of the Lord Jesus, how he said, It is more blessed to give than to receive.*

Know you are rich and give generously, trusting in My abundance
Entertain no scrimpy thought when it comes to matters of finance
Give, give, give; My Love will see you through every encumbrance
You belong to the Owner of the earth and in Him is your inheritance

Mighty is your Power, for you are My working hands to save My world
Hold nothing back of time, comfort, and care; prove you are concerned
For the needy, the hungry, the poor and lost, it is they who are preferred
Love, support, reach out in peace, wipe their tears; let none get spurned

## August 31

## Take Action

**Psalm 96:3**
*Declare his glory among the heathen, his wonders among all people.*

Yours eternally is a home in Heaven; save others, take action
A life of prayer in communion with Me will reveal My salvation
Deny yourself, take up My cross to fulfill My Great Commission
And it is essential to pray and fast; keep Me in communication

I know that fasting is not what you wanted to hear me advocate
But in some situations, it is the only way, and you cannot delegate
You must still call on the Lord and pray, perhaps with an associate
Make sure it is the Lord who is in control, to Him your fast dedicate

# September

## September 1

## I Give You My All

**Romans 14:23**
*[F]or whatsoever is not from faith is sin.*

Down the ages, none can deny My unfailing Love for it is proven
"I will never leave you nor forsake you," is dependable, not illusion
Think, what does it mean? Not just My Presence, My *all* is given
Grace, understanding, strength, and patience, yours in our union

My children, be ever sure My Love cannot deny you any resource
My tireless patience, the strength you need, I Am your warhorse!
You are always understood; I know you as no one does, of course!
So how can you fear a future full of promise? Isn't that ridiculous?

Your heavenly Father hears, pities your fears, knows your wants
Meets your needs, only your blind demands He delays or grants
It is best if your prayers all merge into one, becoming constants
"Thy will be done." Know His great Heart keeps His covenants

## September 2

## Divine Assurance

**Isaiah 25:1**

*O LORD, thou art my God; I will exalt thee, I will praise thy name;*
*for thou hast done wonderful things; thy counsels of old are faithfulness*
*and truth.*

If I Am truly Lord, it is enough for Me to command your obedience
Loyal service is your role, mine to protect you with My Presence
I plan for you and secure the needed resources; do you need evidence?
To doubt My provision is to deny My faithfulness and My guidance

When fears beset, always declare God is Love; check every dread
Show Me a grateful spirit, your ever-trusting heart, and a cool head
So carry no woes, shed no tears; all is bliss, for My Love is assured
Wonders await ahead; My grace divine encircles all for My beloved

## September 3

## Nobody Can Snatch

**Deuteronomy 33:27**
*The eternal God is thy refuge, and underneath are the everlasting arms: and he shall thrust out the enemy from before thee; and shall say, Destroy them.*

Worry, misery, depression, want and woe, faintness, and heartache
These can be sin's avatars carrying deadly poison like a rattlesnake
They seem mild or fleeting, but they can overcome you and remake
I Am your Savior from everything weighing you down, each mistake

You are a spirit-being clothed in flesh, your real Life in the unseen
Let not earth's woes or seductions derail your journey in between
Consider why I put you in a place of testing; what does it all mean?
Lift your heads, stand in awe of My glories and sing a victory paean

Take My joy deep within your soul and relinquish your burdens to Me
If you continue to be troubled, you have reclaimed your load foolishly

Losing trust in My Presence for a minute, and you cannot be carefree
Underneath My everlasting arms, to snatch you away, there is nobody

## September 4

## Cast Your Burden

**Psalm 68:19**

*Blessed be the Lord, who daily loadeth us with benefits, even the God of our salvation. Selah.*

I Am your Peace even if all goes wrong; rely on Me, cast your burden
In stormy seas, I will walk on water; in Me, there is nothing to frighten
Sail away rejoicing, worry not, the wind may howl, let it not dishearten
Lift your eyes, not to the dark clouds above, but to your Savior, listen

I Am your burden-bearer; I take the weight your tired soul cannot bear
To deal with them as each load requires and I make them all disappear
When deceived by dread and doubt your trust in My promises are unclear
You are not sure what to do; you think God is not answering and you fear

## September 5

## Love God and Neighbor

**Luke 10:27**

*And he answering said, Thou shalt love the Lord thy God with all thy heart, and with all thy soul, and with all thy strength, and with all thy mind; and thy neighbour as thyself.*

I have decreed and designed you to grow in Me and rise higher
Life, beauty, knowledge, and power are yours making you wiser
Progress begins with your rebirth; in My Kingdom, it is the order
Loving God and neighbor My two commandments will empower

Do not allow pride or unforgiveness to keep you apart in separation
That is the most effective way to grow and gain My divine direction
For meaning and purpose in life, you will find no better instruction
Day to day increasing in favor with God and man with conviction

## September 6

## Eternity Not Oblivion

**1 Corinthians 15:54**
*So when this corruptible shall have put on incorruption, and this mortal shall have put on immortality, then shall be brought to pass the saying that is written, Death is swallowed up in victory. O death,*
*where is thy sting? O grave, where is thy victory?*

Your departed loved one's dwell in the ecstasy of My Presence
Do not fret; their happiness is beyond any earthly experience
The afterlife is not oblivion; isn't My Resurrection the evidence?
No one is idle in Paradise; you grow in My Love and significance

As angels ministered to Me when on earth with no human witness
So loved ones, unseen, now free of fleshly restraints, pray to bless
They plead your cause in My Presence; for they have direct access
Compassed about with a great cloud of witnesses, tarry, blameless

When it is time for you to join your dear ones rejoicing in My divinity
All evil, suffering and sorrow there are washed away in perpetuity
Where My joy is the air you breathe, discover Kingdom life in reality
Knowing Life eternal is Father, Son, and Holy Spirit, one God in Trinity

In Me, draw near to eternity and earth's troubles and sorrows diminish
Focus far away, look at things unseen but more real; they will astonish
Only I can keep loved ones from oblivion; they pray for you, not vanish
One day all earthly relationships end, but in Me, they continue to flourish

## September 7

## Your Hiding Place

**Psalm 32:7**

*Thou art my hiding place; thou shalt preserve me from trouble; thou shalt compass me about with songs of deliverance. Selah.*

I Am your hiding place, harbor in the storm, where none can bother
The eternal God is your refuge; He is tender, your heavenly Father
Let the reality of His protection sink into your soul; look no further
He alone keeps you from all harm; He is Almighty God and Creator

My Father's sovereign Love gave you sanctuary, free amazing grace
A plan that seems like folly to many, to rescue the fallen human race
When life's storms hurl thunderbolts that terrify and daunt your face
Joyful in His refuge, fearless, say it aloud, Jesus is your hiding place

## September 8

## Walk in My Love

**1 Timothy 6:10**

*For the love of money is the root of all evil: which while some coveted*
*after, they have erred from the faith, and pierced themselves through*
*with many sorrows.*

My supply can never fail, but at times, I will test your conviction
Do you trust Me, or do you hoard? Has money become an addiction?
Show Me; to someone in difficulty, go and make a generous contribution
Let go and manage wealth as a trusted steward; it will end stagnation

Your giving, not keeping, frees your spirit; it allows My supply to flow
It tells me your heart is trusting, you submit your will to Me and grow
What a relief to have My Peace and Joy when you obey Me and follow
The love of money is the root of all evil; it will keep you in the shallow

I know it is hard to imagine My Love and Care; one day, when you know
You are the apple of My eye; you will rejoice like you never have before

In the meantime, observe the difference in the lives of those
who follow
They walk with a triumphant spring in their step as if there is
no tomorrow

## September 9

## After the Crucible

**Proverbs 27:21**
*As the fining pot for silver, and the furnace for gold; so is a man to his praise.*

When you genuinely come to Life in Me, there can be no failure
That can only happen if you lose hope, give up, and surrender
Overcome by challenges I send to build you? Praise, do not fear
In My Hand, I hold the world; dominate all you dread; I Am near

The success you seek in life must be according to My specification
Not that of the world; for authentic success is only in My Redemption
Deemed a failure on earth, perhaps, but mine is a different evaluation
Your reward is assured, for I define progress with another definition

Win souls, heal the sick, cast out devils, sacrifice or love your enemies
The world does not care about such issues; it scorns all these activities
But for Me, your risen Savior, these count; they must be your legacies
The Joys of observing the great spiritual truths unfold are not banalities

The world is blind to My revelation; the heavens open only to the humble

Discard your vanity; in the essential task of renewal, you must
not fumble
It is the priority I first tackle; when I Am weeding or pruning,
don't crumble
I assign you to major assignments only after I get you out of the
crucible

## September 10

## Do Not Be Deluded

**Matthew 6:24**

*No man can serve two masters: for either he will hate the one, and love the other; or else he will hold to the one, and despise the other. Ye cannot serve God and Mammon.*

You cannot have your cake and eat it, too; the world and I are apart
My Word is specific; if you serve Mammon, you ask God to depart
Those who try to claim wages from both foolishly try to outsmart
You can have complete satisfaction in Me; think it over, and restart

I require your complete allegiance; I do not hold a divided command
When you let Mammon seduce you, then you comply with his demand
You will lose control of your heart and your mind; do you understand
Deluded, you will turn from God to a deity leading you into quicksand

Money, prestige, and power are idols worshipped by all his protégées
Trappings that try to hide the deformity of pride that marks Pharisees

In My Kingdom, your Life in Me restrains the lust of the eyes for these
All the resources and rewards you need, I lovingly supply My devotees

## September 11

## A Generous Giver

**John 15:5**

*I Am the vine, ye are the branches: He that abideth in me, and I in him, the same bringeth forth much fruit: for without me ye can do nothing.*

Taste of My abundant Life; it is yours to harvest in ample measure
To give you eternal Life is why I came to rescue you, My treasure
In your Lord and Master's unmatched generosity, you are secure
Let your mind, heart, and soul pulsate with joy; live, never unsure

"I Am the Vine, and ye are the branches," is about how the sap flows
My Life, too, streamed through you, entwines us, even as it hallows
Thus, our lives are one, and everything that is in Me in you overflows
Nine fruit of the Spirit and more; all your Lord and Savior bestows

Love, joy, peace, patience, kindness, generosity, and faithfulness
All are My precious gifts, not forgetting self-control and gentleness
If you strive to acquire these attributes, they will cause you no stress
When My Life flows through you, I start your transformation process

## September 12

## On Solid Rock

**1 Samuel 12:24**
*Only fear the LORD, and serve him in truth with all your heart: for consider how great things he hath done for you.*

Single-minded, seek My Kingdom to serve, and you live in My light
Unbending, secure your will, eyes steadfast on God's glory and might
Your burning desire that My Kingdom come, your anticipated delight
With a life bent only on serving and advancing My dominion forthright

Harbor not the values of the world; true profit is only in spiritual gain
Whatever you achieve in life, ensure My Kingdom is what you proclaim
Abandon the love of money altogether; and seek My service, not acclaim
Build on solid rock, not on sinking sand; make a difference, ignore fame

## September 13

## No Other Name

**Jeremiah 29:12**
*Then shall ye call upon me, and ye shall go and pray unto me,*
*And I will harken unto you.*

Dominate evil in the Power of My Name; no other power can overcome
Evil spirits, hearing the sound of Jesus, panic; for them, it is fearsome
In weakness, fear, sorrow, or pain, call My Name; you will find asylum
For My Name means Salvation, your crucified Redeemer, the only One

Often you call your earthly mother; when we connect, it is My delight
You want your mother's comfort or care, especially if you get a fright
Just like her, I know you by name; and you are never out of My sight
When in trouble, or even if you are fine, call Me to say you are alright

## September 14

## The Cry of Faith

**Romans 1:17**
*For therein is the righteousness of God revealed from Faith to Faith:*
*as it is written, the just shall live by Faith.*

My compassion for all is the same today as when I was on earth
For Me, faults and failings can never change your priceless worth
Humble cries for help show Faith, trusting Me in your new birth
You are learning that My Power is for you, as Faith grows in girth

Every soul with authentic life in Me will, in Faith, admit helplessly
Crying, "Lord, I believe. Help Thou mine unbelief," simultaneously
Making an honest plea for My Power to overcome unbelief completely
It is an appeal I never ignore, whenever My children are seeking Me

## September 15

## Why Do You Fear?

**Psalm 18:2**
*The Lord is my rock, and my fortress, and my deliverer; my God, my strength, in whom I will trust; my buckler, and the horn of my salvation, and my high tower.*

"In quietness and confidence shall be your strength." It is about rest
My Life-giving Power ebbs and flows in stillness and calm, not stress
Strength in My Kingdom is quietness and peace, not actions reckless
I call you to My Rest; a veiled future is not to be feared; I will bless

You have refuge in a Savior; step out in freedom, boldly do My Will
A promise of marvelous contentment, My Peace and Joy, will I instill
Not a problem left unsolved; Prayer for all you need, and I will fulfill
When I Am your stronghold, what is there to fear? In Peace, be still!

## September 16

## Seasons

**Acts 14:17**

*Nevertheless he left not himself without witness, in that he did good, and*
*gave us rain from heaven, and fruitful seasons, filling our hearts with*
*food and gladness.*

In Me, Life can ebb and flow in My Peace that passes all understanding
The world is fickle, helter-skelter, but remember, My Love is reassuring
Like a river meandering through dry land, bringing new life, it is reviving
But it flows in seasons, and times of trouble can also precede My blessing

Working in peace and calm is rewarding, for it results in the best outcome
Nothing in haste, living in Me, you live in eternity; time is not the fulcrum
I have planned your future; rest in My Love, and nothing can overcome
Being fruitful in My service counts, not what the world thinks is awesome

## September 17

### The Way to Walk

**1 Kings 19:12**

*And after the earthquake a fire; but the LORD was not in the fire: and*
*after the fire a still small voice.*

Listen for that still, small voice telling you this is the way to walk
The narrow road, the uncertainty ahead, knowing I Am your rock
Fearless about the future, confident I Am leading you, not just talk
It is My Way; trust My promise that all is well; I protect My flock

## September 18

## No Tourists

**Psalm 63:7–8**
*For you are my deliverer; under your wings, I rejoice.*
*My soul pursues you; your right hand upholds me.*

Once in My sanctuary, no power on earth can do you any harm
But do not be a tourist; only permanent residents have no qualm
Come to dwell, not for erratic visits, and receive Gilead's balm
My beloved children, in My hiding place, you have eternal calm

You rest in the shadow of My wings where nothing can intrude
Safe in My grip, protected from stormy winds of any magnitude
Fears assail you only if you stop trusting My Word and exclude
Hurry back into My shelter; it is folly to venture into servitude

## September 19

## A Treasure Overlooked

**Isaiah 58:14**

*Then you will find joy in your relationship to the LORD, and I will*
*give you great prosperity, and cause crops to grow on the land I gave*
*to your ancestor Jacob. Know for certain that the LORD has spoken.*

My Truths that you receive are the same as My disciples received
Joy in abundance is My intent, in fulness obtained if fully believed
I want your lives to overflow with My Joy; it is not quite perceived
It is an overlooked treasure worth hunting; you will not get deceived

## September 20

## It Is All Part of Life

**Deuteronomy 20:3**

*And shall say unto them, Hear, O Israel, ye approach this day unto battle against your enemies: let not your hearts faint, fear not, and do not tremble, neither be ye terrified because of them.*

Trust your heavenly Father's goodness, leave everything in His care
Past, Present and Future are in His hands, be sure nothing can snare
Praise Him constantly; tell all people God is good; many are unaware
Evil He erases, chaos He calms, turns panic to Peace, go and declare!

My Father and I are one, and our intent is only the best for our children
Help you share in our goodness and eliminate your fears of the hidden
Teach you to trust and not be frightened of troubles that arise and burden
It is all part of life's training we have designed to build you and embolden

## September 21

## My Father and I

**John 20:28–29**

*And Thomas answered and said unto him, My Lord and my God.*
*Jesus saith unto him, Thomas, because thou hast seen me,*
*thou hast believed: blessed are they that have not seen, and*
*yet have believed.*

My Disciples thought they had not seen My Heavenly Father
I was with them long enough for them to know their Teacher
My Father and I are One; their ignorance was a bit of a bother
Knowing Me, they'd know My Father, but they couldn't decipher

My children, the Apostle Thomas, had his doubts; what about you?
After seeing My nail-scarred hands, he believed, what is your view?
Your belief in the Father, Son, and Holy Spirit trust and often renew
And to Three Persons in One God, forge your prayers and worldview

God your Creator, Jesus your Savior, and the Holy Spirit your Guide
Love, Strength, and Beauty the same is in all in the Trinity you abide
Trusting and serving one God humbly proclaim His essence ratified
Savor His peace, and live in serenity, Love and Joy abundant beside

## September 22

## Sing Praises

**Psalm 47:6**
*Sing praises to God, sing praises: sing praises unto our King, sing praises.*

Convey the love of your glad heart with a praise offering
Reveal the depths of your Faith in every tribute you bring
Praise My Holy Name, and in every minute of the day sing
With the heavenly Host to the ruler of the world, your King

Gladly may your voices ring with thankful songs of praise
To Father, Son, and Holy Spirit for their redeeming grace
Magnify your Savior, Priest, and King; His Love embrace
For Christ, the Lamb of God came for your eternal solace

## September 23

## I Draw Nigh

**James 4:8**

*Draw nigh to God, and he will draw nigh to you. Cleanse your hands, ye sinners; and purify your hearts, ye double-minded.*

You have My Word, turn to Me, to you then, will I draw nigh
Take the initiative, and you become conscious I Am nearby
Turn to Me in gratitude for answered prayer or a frantic cry
Whatever your circumstances are, be sure I Am standing by

You need not come as a supplicant; I sense your mute appeal
Your longing reaches My heart; no gifts or pleading, no ordeal
Know the wonder of My Love, ask, and receive; that is the deal
Praise your heavenly Father, tell of His goodness, do not conceal

In His Love, He gives all the gifts you need and cannot measure
Joyfully He blesses you, and that brings Him so much pleasure
It is not only His readiness to help, but His nature is your treasure
Give Him complete devotion; cast all your cares, live in His power

## September 24

## What's Your Answer?

**John 6:68**
*Lord, to whom shall we go? Thou hast the words of Eternal Life.*

I Am your Great Teacher; all Truth must point to Me; and no other
Simon Peter accredited the words of eternal life to Me, his Master
When I said, no one can come to Me unless granted by My Father
Some of My disciples left, and I asked the twelve for their answer

They had come to believe in Me, the Christ, Son of the living God
Do you believe in Me? My Word is Life, fear not, abide in your Lord
Let Me design your life and give you the right directions, not flawed
I do not impose My Way. You are free; choose your very own method

## September 25

## My Rest Embrace

**Joshua 21:44**
*And the LORD gave them rest round about, according to all that he sware unto their fathers: and there stood not a man of all their enemies before them; the LORD delivered all their enemies into their hand.*

I did not design your life to be hectic; it is My peace you need
But make no doctor's visits, come to abide, not only to intercede
Assured of My help, rest and wait until all your worries recede
Feel the thrill of My Presence and know in Me you will succeed

Resting in Me, do not succumb to fear; savor My Love and Grace
Let your heart overflow with joy and delight, eyes fixed on My face
Concerned for no want, bold and confident in life's demanding race
Breathe God's fresh air, feel His refreshing rain and His rest embrace

## September 26

## Humble Service

**Isaiah 57:15**

*For thus saith the high and lofty One that inhabiteth eternity, whose*
*name is Holy; I dwell in the high and holy place, with him also that is*
*of a contrite and humble spirit, to revive the spirit of the humble, and*
*to revive the heart of the contrite ones.*

Loving service to all proves your Sonship; people are My priority
Honor all who cross your path, not just those in your community
As guests in My Father's house, show them love and sensitivity
No person or labor is beneath you; serve at every opportunity

Joyful in doing My Will, glad in My service, serving all constantly
Remember, you are My steward; I count on you to work faithfully
Your Savior washed His disciples' feet; then I died for humanity
Humbly serving others, I expect you too, must show your Love for Me

## September 27

## Divine Ordeal

**Numbers 11:23**
*And the LORD said unto Moses, Is the LORD'S hand waxed short?*
*Thou shalt see now whether my word shall come to pass unto thee or not.*

My Power to save grows with your understanding of My Salvation
The new birth in Me is Union, and for you, there is no condemnation
Free from sin's power, you experience the mystery of transformation
In all your failures, My Hand extends to rescue you from any situation

My saving Power is unlimited, but man's free will and vision matter
Hope for a better future comes with a vision; lack of it can counter
My desire and longing to give you My abundant Life is the clincher
Fear not; My hand is not short; I will see you through, whatever

I cherish your rights as an individual; never do I enforce My decree
Salvation is free, when souls spurn My Love, it is very hard to see
My longing and divine impatience to redeem reminds Me of Calvary

But I must wait till a soul gives Me the right, accepts My guarantee

Waiting for that decision is an ordeal, for My Love brooks no delay
Oh, that souls would claim My miracle-working Power, swiftly obey
My longing, loving Heart hurts to see you in pain and life in disarray
When all you have to do is call for My help to take your sins away

## September 28

## The Secret Path

**Isaiah 53:3**

*He is despised and rejected of men; a man of sorrows, and acquainted with grief: and we hid as it were our faces from him; he was despised,*
*and we esteemed him not.*

Obedience and an ordinary life marked My three-year earth Mission
Experiencing hardship and discipline of humanity with no exception
A sinless life, but no different than what was My people's condition
Share the sufferings of My broken world; do not try to live in isolation

I shared in human suffering, so what was true of Me must be of you
"He saved others. Himself He cannot save," was said of Me; it is true
Do not be blind to the plight of lost souls; join in My Mission to rescue
You have learned of My perfect Way; go tell the world what to pursue

Follow Me, the Man of Sorrows, on a path for My nearest and dearest
Called to save and share in a way I reserve for seekers of the highest

Ready to surrender, sacrifice and count all things loss to gain
My fullest
If My work seems dull versus the world's excitement, you miss
the best

## September 29

## I Want You to Soar

**Psalm 28:8**

*The Lord is their strength, and he is the saving strength of his anointed.*

Be still before Me as I lay My hand on your head, let My Spirit flow
My healing touch has ancient power, gently curing all your sorrow
I guide you individually with My Hand, be at peace about tomorrow
In whatever situation you may be, remember you are in My shadow

I Am your fortress and refuge; wait on Me, your strength, to restore
You have the promise of My Power; like the eagle, I want you to soar
Let not your heart be troubled; the future is in My hand; I do not ignore
Pure sweet Peace you find in My tower, your Lord; you humbly adore

## September 30

## You Will Persevere

**1 John 4:18**
*There is no fear in love; but perfect love casteth out fear: because fear hath torment. He that feareth is not made perfect in love.*

My strength is promised to you day by day; nothing should you fear
Confront each hardship confidently in My Power; you will persevere
Trust your promise-keeping Lord in every necessity; I Am very near
If I give you a task to complete, the provision you need will be there

Why dread, and why doubt? Is it because you do not trust what I say?
Ask Me for strength when you need it; instead, you worry, do not obey
Get free of panic and stress in My Love; all your nagging doubts slay
Surrender your life to God for joy and peace, and do not be helpless prey

# October

## October 1

## Profitable Desert Time

**Exodus 14:21**
*And Moses stretched out his hand over the sea; and the LORD caused the sea to go back by a strong east wind all that night, and made the sea dry land, and the waters were divided.*

Your Salvation comes from no other source; look to Me alone
Know I Am your Jehovah Jireh, your Provider; I Am the only One
In ignorance, many languish in needless scarcity, for their scorn
Share My faithfulness with all in distress; make Me widely known

Whoever has the keys to My storehouse is entitled to claim supply
Your humble trust in My Word tugs at My heart; know I will satisfy
Is it a crisis or a desire to help others? Come to Me; I will not deny
But if you prefer to worry and doubt, not believe, how can I comply?

I provided manna and meat for the children of Israel in the wilderness
Pursued by the Egyptians, I tore apart the Red Sea in their great distress
Their suffering I exchanged for milk and honey of Canaan's goodness
Time in the desert is profitable; in repentance and trust is your success

## October 2

### See the Difference?

**Matthew 21:5**

*Tell ye the daughter of Sion, Behold, thy King cometh unto thee, meek, and sitting upon an ass, and a colt the foal of an ass.*

Look back on years gone by and fairly evaluate your times of stress
Wasn't the going rough only whenever you did something reckless?
Ignored My leading, chose to go your way and gave in to weakness
Perhaps led by someone you knew, you joined in some foolishness

Now consider the times you followed My leading; see the difference?
You were stress-free, sensitive to the touch of My hand, in obedience
Not choosing your defiant, unruly way, but My Will in every instance
Trusting Me with heart and soul, giving up control without resistance

Does My Word, "The meek shall inherit the earth," sound exaggerated?
See that attribute, not as an indication of weakness but a mind exalted
To follow Me meekly in cheerful accord and delight is My Power activated

The genuinely meek are more skilled at ruling others, even if understated

Meek is about living, yielding, and conquering; it reflects your inheritance
Filled in My Spirit's power and every waking hour by seeking My guidance
Hallmark of a yielded Will obeying My decrees and commands in cadence
Broken are chains of the yoke you wore, now walking free in My Presence

## October 3

## Unconditional Favor

**Isaiah 32:17**

*The work of righteousness shall be Peace, and the effect of righteousness*
*quietness and assurance for ever.*

Rest and live in Me; Everything about you will communicate My calm
If you learn to be still and know I Am God, fixed in My Love, no qualm
Attain that repose to get My work done, ready for the world's bedlam
Your body and soul are strong enough to conquer, unafraid of any harm

My righteousness you have obtained, for I redeemed you at Calvary
But My Peace is in right living to experience My support and serenity
Enslaved no more to sin and pride, resting in My favor, unconditionally
Humble and calmly confident, knowing you cannot live like a Pharisee

## October 4

## Your Fulfillment

**Psalm 139:14**
*I will praise thee; for I Am fearfully and wonderfully made: marvelous are thy works; and that my soul knoweth right well.*

My Spirit-guided children think differently from the crowd
But those who do not care to know Me choose to be proud
Nothing in Me appeals to them; for worldly allures are loud
For those who do know me, nothing could be more hallowed

I do not paint on a proud canvas, but you are My masterpiece
My exclusive work of art, but if ruled by pride, you have no part
The Joy of knowing Me can never find a residence in your heart
My portrait will remain unfinished because of your ego's thwart

Draw near and see Me as I truly am; your heart's one big desire
Your Savior who plucked you out of the hands of the destroyer
Who knit you fearfully and wonderfully in Love to draw you nearer
I Am the perfection of all that you long for and to which you aspire

# October 5

## My Work of Art

**Titus 3:7**

*That being justified by his grace, we should be made heirs according*
*to the hope of eternal life.*

When in My care, whatever you do, whoever you meet, I Am at the helm
That means nothing is coincidental, and with Me, there is no overwhelm
I assign people who cross your path no chance meetings in My realm
All planned, all blessed, no condemnation, only help with any problem

My children, you are My heirs, and your heritage you cannot disinherit
Led by My Spirit, you are the sons of God; it is a gift not based on merit
Sharing in My sufferings, you will share in My glory; that is My holy writ
People are My work of art; the only clay I sculpt, for in you is My true grit

The purpose of suffering is your waking from the dead for divine integration
You will be perfect like your heavenly Father, in Me alone is a sacred union

Transformed to My likeness, evidence of Sonship, it is our eternal communion
Oh, what rapture and mystery, and all because of My death and Resurrection!

## October 6

## I Hold the Outcome

**Psalm 138:7**
*Though I walk in the midst of trouble, thou wilt revive me: thou shalt stretch forth thine hand against the wrath of mine enemies, and thy right hand shall save me.*

Enduring Faith that does not let go in any situation gets rewarded
Like a child's tiny hand in yours, complete trust for being guarded
That is how My heart is; like any protective parent, I, too, feel loved
Musn't such confidence evoke a response and indeed be commended?

You are battle-scarred and helpless, with no help in sight and desperate
I long for you to turn and take My hand, but often you behave obstinate
Your free will prevents Me from canceling your choices that degenerate
Life is a crucible; the refining process gets longer if you are insubordinate

You would not fail a little child seeking help regardless of circumstances
I created you; would My Love ignore My children's helpless utterances?
Fear not; I've promised never to forsake you, whatever the disturbances

Never doubt I will stop at nothing to rescue you from all your grievances

You have a course to follow; trust Me to be the person you must become
I know every Cross you carry, the battles you fight, sins to be overcome
Secure in My arms, be sure of My protection, know My might is fearsome
Do not fear the future, but do not let go of My hand; for I hold the outcome

## October 7

## The Only Failure

**Mark 9:23–24**

*Jesus said unto him, If thou canst believe, all things are possible to him that believeth. And straightway the father of the child cried out,*
*and said with tears, Lord, I believe; help thou mine unbelief.*

Lord, I believe, the man cried, help thou my unbelief, his heartfelt prayer
Could I ever ignore that? No cry for My help escapes My ears; I deeply care
Every plea, sigh, or worry or cry, "Lord; my many failings won't you spare?"
In all your hardship and sorrows, turn to Me; I Am longing for you to share

Do not be ashamed of your weaknesses; in them is My strength perfected
Rejoice in My Love and understanding; do not let them make you dejected
You may fear, but I Am there to protect you, and you won't be disappointed
The only failure is when you doubt Me; for your mind gets contaminated

## October 8

## The Dark Places

**Isaiah 43:2**

*When thou passest through the waters, I will be with thee; and through*
*the rivers, they shall not overflow thee: when thou walkest through the*
*fire, thou shalt not be burned; neither shall the flame kindle upon thee.*

When the mere thought of Me makes you glad, brings Joy and conviction
That is the heart I seek, genuine Love for Me with faithful contemplation
Think often of Me for healing from all your sorrows, for every depression
Physical, mental, or spiritual needs bring them to Me for transformation

Doubts and fears may come during life's fierce storms; will you despair?
Know I Am always ready to help, but observing whether you easily scare
Is My glad Presence enough, or will you let powers of darkness ensnare?
In all your ups and downs, remember no blight can overcome in My care

Keep your Joy and courage of conviction; let not the heart's strings snap

Do not worry about facing hardship; know that My Love is not a stopgap
I will not let you climb mountains alone; beside you, I will never draw back
You are to rejoice before the Lord your God in everything, and not fall back

## October 9

## Your Impatient Lover

**Ephesians 3:17–19**
*That Christ may dwell in your hearts by faith; that ye, being rooted*
*and grounded in love, may be able to comprehend with all saints*
*what is the breadth, and length, and depth, and height; And to know*
*the love of Christ, which passeth knowledge, that ye might be filled*
*with all the fulness of God.*

You are familiar with portrayals of mortal love; most are counterfeit
Human relationships are incapable of true devotion, would you admit?
It is Divine Love men and women long to experience but do not get it
Including Me would make all the difference; too many think I do not fit

Love is a many splendored thing, but in flesh, you only get a foretaste
Without Me, people fall in and out of love all the time; it is such a waste
If only they'd realize I'm no killjoy but the essential spice in perfect taste
I designed Love as a magnet to draw you to Me, not mere flesh in haste

How I long for your Love, as your Savior from sin's burden and despair

Your impatient Lover, waiting to rescue and take you into My loving care
Gladly receiving your demands for help as My beloved's rights in prayer
Insisting I get involved in your joys and sorrows, in ties of Love we share

## October 10

## Be a Good Steward

**1 Corinthians 3:13**
*Every man's work shall be made manifest: for the day shall declare it,*
*because it shall be revealed by fire; and the fire shall try every man's*
*work of what sort it is.*

Anticipate My blessings at the end of every challenge in life's journey
You know I Am walking with you, and in trust, you press on confidently
Knowing every obstacle and everyone in your path is sent to you by Me
Being a good steward, gladly serving as you would expect others to be

Don't you get tired of a self-indulgent lazy servant who shuns his work?
He ill-serves you, neglecting his duties; his complaints drive you berserk
Does that aptly describe your service to Me? Yet you expect every perk!
Think it over when you gripe and grumble; how do I feel when you shirk?

## October 11

## The Secret of Praise

**Psalm 22:26**
*The meek shall eat and be satisfied: they shall praise the Lord that seek him: your heart shall live for ever.*

My children, unlock the secret to overcoming even in great distress
When difficulties abound, the key is Praise, remembering My goodness
Look back, count every blessing you have received, faithfully witness
Use no other strategy to ask for My help; and bind it with thankfulness

There is no need to be overwhelmed; only trust, be sure of deliverance
Our relationship, once established, is permanent; it is your inheritance
Even if your distress is self-inflicted, it matters not, but end disobedience
Everything is under My power, but free will comes under your dominance

You must do your part to escape Satan's snares, and I will surely do mine
Fears, worries, and troubles, I use all to instruct; he uses them to entwine

Your troubles and tears are a prelude to My rest; a guarantee that is divine
But get right with Me; obtaining My forgiveness is not exacting discipline

## October 12

## Thrill of Souls Saved

**Romans 3:3–4**

*For what if some did not believe? shall their unbelief make the faith of*
*God without effect? God forbid: yea, let God be true, but every man a*
*liar; as it is written, That thou mightest be justified in thy sayings, and*
*mightest overcome when thou art judged.*

You are grateful for My gift of Salvation but know I Am so thankful too
Our Heavenly Father's gift is your redemption, but My inheritance is you
In Calvary's agony, the thrill of saving souls stayed with Me all through
At Gethsemane, I pleaded for the cup to pass; My Father's Will, I knew

My disciples performed no miracles at the time, as they would eventually
Fearless after My Resurrection, they boldly proclaimed My Name faithfully
That is what I expect; are you doers of My Word or just hearers nominally?
Dedication in all you do, minor or marvel, delights My Heart continuously

## October 13

## Setbacks Don't Count

**Romans 5:7–8**

*For scarcely for a righteous man will one die: yet peradventure for a*
*good man some would even dare to die. But God commendeth his love*
*toward us, in that, while we were yet sinners, Christ died for us.*

The power of praise, I revealed; the plea to believe I will never ignore
Great Faith will be yours, increasing to an extent you never had before
In your new understanding, you will look back at your unbelief to deplore
Steady growth is the hallmark of My Kingdom; your progress I care for

In Me is no stagnation, growth, strength, and power from glory to glory
Eternal is the promise of My abundant Life; it is reality; it is not a theory
Failures or setbacks do not count; only lessons learned, not old memory
Its use is only as rungs of My Kingdom ladders, shaped in life's factory

Rungs of sorrow, failure, or success matter only to serve their purpose
Keep climbing, disregard each bar and step up, do not be self-conscious

On My secure ladder, you will not fall unless you choose to be iniquitous
I gave you free will; if you step off, My love for you remains continuous

But bounce back on your journey no matter how far you may step away
Lost in the world, remember it is never too late to make amends and pray
You were adrift but not alone; in looking for My sheep, I take no holiday
Like the Prodigal, escape from sin's grip into Father's loving arms today

## October 14

## The Bargain

**John 1:29**

*The next day John seeth Jesus coming unto him, and saith, Behold the*
*Lamb of God, which taketh away the sin of the world.*

The Lamb of God takes away the sins of the world; I said, "It is finished"
Hanging on to your past mocks My Passover sacrifice; it gets diminished
Now all you do is cast your burdens on Me, go live your life astonished
Yes, it is a mystery; Past, Present and Future sins forgiven, extinguished

After repentance, if you dwell on the past, you make My death worthless
I do not remember your dirty sins; I cleansed your filth in My forgiveness
You are free, do not lock your soul in jail for yourself, for that is madness
Neither chain anyone in your cell unforgiven; it will rob all your happiness

My death for your Life, an exchange. Is that a little simpler to explain?
To end man's bondage to evil, I was the sinless sacrifice, the one bargain

The Mediator for humanity reconciling God and man is what I became
To redeem you from sin to My Resurrected Life immortal, in My domain

## October 15

## Plenty or Poverty

**Romans 8:6**
*For to be carnally minded is death; but to be spiritually minded is life and peace.*

I Am your hiding place; in Me, find safety and complete satisfaction
Divine abundance is infinite; My storehouses are never in depletion
If you are not convinced you will remain uncertain of My provision
Once you are sure of this you will realize its material manifestation

Lack of supply should never be your concern; as the heirs of a King
Confident of My sufficiency live, work and progress fearing nothing
Use prosperity for good stewardship, increasing talents by investing
Plenty or poverty both can indicate your obedience and My blessing

# October 16

## The Vital Weapon

**Psalm 43:5**

*Why art thou cast down, O my soul? and why art thou disquieted within me? hope in God: for I shall yet praise him, who is the health*
*of my countenance, and my God.*

Praise can change your most challenging situations into My Joy
It can transform your life, the vital weapon in prayer you employ
Turn your unrest into rest, turmoil to trust, and your fears destroy
Break chains of error and bondage, unleash My praise to redeploy

## October 17

## Panic to Peace

**Philippians 4:8**

*Finally, brethren, whatsoever things are true, whatsoever things are honest, whatsoever things are just, whatsoever things are pure, whatsoever things are lovely, whatsoever things are of good report; If*
*there be any virtue, and if there be any praise, think on these things.*

Shield your eyes from squalid surroundings in your vicinity
I created a world full of beauty, do not lose your sensitivity
In the ugliness and defects, you see, maintain your identity
Let Faith will keep your vision on My purposes and priority

What is the power of My Resurrection if not transformation?
Bringing beauty from deformity and calm from the commotion
Taking you from panic to Peace, and anguish to appreciation
In the fellowship of My sufferings, making you a new creation

As I Am with My Father, you can now aspire to tasks that are greater
The limitations on the earth that I walked on as a man are now fewer
To witness and save souls, resources and technology are far superior
Ask, and I will readily grant you access to My miracle-working Power

## October 18

## Until You Fail

**Mark 14:49–50**

*I was daily with you in the temple teaching, and ye took me not: but the*
*scriptures must be fulfilled. And they all forsook him and fled.*

My disciples forsook Me and fled, they left Me in pain and loneliness
But down the ages, My follower's zeal to serve certifies to their witness
Father did not forsake Me on the Cross; I fulfilled scripture in righteousness
My sin atonement could not taint My Holy Father's standard of sinlessness

My cry, "My God, My God, why have you forsaken Me?" has many awed
It is about God's hatred of sin, and to suggest His abandoning Me is fraud
At Calvary, I became sin so you could become the righteousness of God
Sin cannot enter God's Presence; to save man My death was the only method

When you feel lonely, desolate, and abandoned, know that I understand
Do not feel discouraged at the sign of trouble, for I will not misunderstand
The Apostles let Me down, but I did not give up on them nor reprimand

Instead, I commissioned them to spread My message all across the land

Those terrified deserters I endowed with Power to heal, raise the dead
I chose primarily poor fishermen, and I ignored the proud and learned
It is failure that teaches you to be meek, rejoice when you are humbled
For My heart is tender and human frailty I pardon when you have fumbled

## October 19

## On Full Alert

**John 1:17**

*For the law was given by Moses, but grace and truth came by Jesus Christ.*

To every cry of a human heart, I have always communicated
I Am on full alert; your cries and My response are integrated
It is an arrangement I delight in and to which I Am committed
Like fine-tuned machine parts working together, not separated

My children, you do not live in a world apart from Me in isolation
You are My priority; I do not deny or meet needs with resignation
I long for your cry in eternity, always waiting to bless your petition
You may not hear Me or respond, but I will never lose our connection

## October 20

## My Yoke Is Easy

**Matthew 11:29–30**

*Take my yoke upon you, and learn of me; for I Am meek and lowly in heart: and ye shall find rest unto your souls. For my yoke is easy, and my burden is light.*

I taught you to pray for My Kingdom and My Will to reign
My Will is the key to the divine inspiration you should gain
To grow in holiness and happiness, you need it to maintain
Your Salvation is My Will; forget your old life; it cannot remain

At the foot of the Cross is Redemption from sin, and freedom
Journey mercies you receive to manage burdens with wisdom
My Will and easy yoke bear on your shoulders in My Kingdom
And step by step, follow Me in Faith and trust in your heirdom

Welcome My Will not only in life's big decisions but in all submit
In every situation and work, small or large, fulfill My divine writ
Be grateful for things you have never considered and make it a habit
Like a rainbow after a storm or a warm winter's day that is sunlit

## October 21

## Imagine the Joy

**Revelation 3:20**
*Behold, I stand at the door, and knock: if any man hear my voice, and open the door, I will come in to him, and will sup with him, and he with me.*

I pursue your heart; My Love is not because of your merit
Know that Salvation is a mystery, a gift; you cannot earn it
You are born from above; eternal life everyone can inherit
All you do is believe and respond to My Love, and you profit

Imagine the Joy of My company at the marriage feast in Cana
Or perhaps at the Last Supper or Emmaus with your Messiah
Sharing any meal with My disciples, you would sing hallelujah
What if I came to your door, and you heard the Voice of Jehovah?

And that is My promise; I will sup with anyone who opens the door
Proud folks excluded; it makes no difference if you are rich or poor
I pour out My Spirit like water, broken cisterns I love all the more
Calling all to My love feast, in the folly of My grace, come anchor

## October 22

## Unshakeable Faith

**Matthew 15:28**

*Then Jesus answered and said unto her, O woman, great is thy faith:*
*be it unto thee even as thou wilt. And her daughter was made whole from that very hour.*

Buttress the ramparts of your soul, build a Faith unshakeable
Stand firm even when you cannot see your way, and be humble
Unable to pray, you feel all hope is gone; trust Me, do not grumble
I renew your mind with My Holy Spirit; you will not be vulnerable

## October 23

### To the Very End

**Hebrews 11:8**
*By faith Abraham, when he was called to go out into a place which he should after receive for an inheritance, obeyed; and he went out, not knowing whither he went.*

Never give up trusting in Me right to the very end in any situation
Alert even when you cannot see what is ahead in whatever condition
Remember, in Faith, Abraham went out, not knowing his relocation
And he was ready to sacrifice Isaac trusting Me for My intervention

All who walk by Faith will face a final test of trust and give evidence
To prove that they count on Me alone, blind to any other interference
Flirting with no other source for succour or some additional assistance
Only relying on the mystery of My provision, living under My guidance

## October 24

## My Keeping Power

**Exodus 25:8**
*And let them make me a sanctuary; that I may dwell among them.*

The power of God keeps the believing soul; it is My commitment
A promise of Joy and beauty in your life despite the environment
Keeping you protected in My impregnable sanctuary as a resident
And living in freedom and sanctity in My Presence that is permanent

Remember the salt of the earth reference in My sermon on the Mount
The keeping power applies to those who consider My Will paramount
Only then is the salt best, its freshness pure, so take that into account
Placed anywhere it stalls corruption; My Purity keeps, for it is the fount

## October 25

## A Conquering Force

**Romans 8:37**
*Nay, in all these things we are more than conquerors through Him that loved us.*

Conquer your self-life within, and you will control the temporal
As My disciple, learn and take command of life, that is corporal
Seek to overcome the material aspects of life, for that is so vital
Take this guidance seriously, engage in conquering the physical

Troublesome situations arise, and gaining sufficiency is important
Do not let the menace of fearing lack make you into its supplicant
Overcome self-life and turn Mammon into a servant from a tyrant
No one would be unemployed if men knew that this is significant

In Me, you are a conquering force; first, overcome the evil in you
After that, see to your home, then work wherever you can renew
When you do, you transform into a force, needed for your sinew
In My Kingdom, overcoming the inner life is what makes you new

## October 26

## Doubters

**John 10:24**
*Then came the Jews round about him, and said unto him, How long dost thou make us to doubt? If thou be the Christ, tell us plainly.*

My Love for you can only accept your total conviction in Me
If you love Me and claim to follow Me, why doubt repeatedly?
The mob spitting in scorn left no scars; I got the third degree
I was hurt by "I know not the man" when Peter forsook Me

And it is the same today; the unbelief of My enemies does not matter
But you who love and know Me can have doubts about your Master
Why are you not sure of Me? Why try checking all options on offer?
Doubting I will keep My promises, are you flirting with the Tempter?

## October 27

## Victory in Each Battle

**1 Corinthians 15:57**
*But thanks be to God, which giveth us the victory through our Lord Jesus Christ.*

Your defects I ignore; I delight in your loving and striving
Though the war rages, each battle won is the victory coming
I do not compare the witness of great saints, even the amazing
For your success, My angels rejoice; I count it as outstanding

## October 28

## Glad Anticipation

**Luke 18:17**

*Verily I say unto you, Whosoever shall not receive the kingdom of God as a little child shall in no wise enter therein.*

Submit to My Will not as if subdued, to accept the inevitable
But in glad anticipation, like a child eager for the memorable
In My Kingdom, only the meek, not the proud, are admissible
Bow in humility and hear My loving Word; know Joy ineffable

## October 29

## Love of Money

**Proverbs 28:22**

*He that hasteth to be rich hath an evil eye, and considereth not that poverty shall come upon him.*

The wealth standard of the world is not for you; choose My wisdom
Love of money is evil, an undeniable way to lose God-given freedom
Set your heart free for things above, for the blessings of My Kingdom
Success, is you revealing My Will and Mind to lost souls; My agendum

## October 30

## Waiting Is Hardest

**Psalm 71:14**
*But I will hope continually, and will yet praise thee more and more.*

Waiting is the most challenging lesson to learn; My Joy is the outcome
Learn to be patient in all things know that My calm is your equilibrium
When you trust Me and submit your will, immediately gain My decorum
From that instant in time, I initiated your eternal Salvation and freedom

There is so much you need to learn to ward off any future misadventure
I stand by you, your Divine Friend sharing in your hardships and failure
My Love is steadfast, My work is perfect, and My ways are just and pure
Walk with Me in faithfulness with all your heart and soul; you will endure

## October 31

## My Transforming Word

**Isaiah 55:11**

*So shall my word be that goeth forth out of my mouth: it shall not return unto me void, but it shall accomplish that which I please, and It*
*shall prosper in the thing whereto I sent it.*

My Word is very life itself, for it is I, your Lord, Savior, and Friend
Study the Scriptures, hide them in your heart against all sin contend
It is a lamp unto your feet, a light to your path for you to transcend
My Voice that touches your hearts, for it is My Grace that I extend

Hearken to My Word, abide in My consciousness free from all fear
Your mind alert to My Holy Spirit whenever temptation draws near
I will create in you a pure heart, and your conscience will be clear
Do not succumb to earthly lusts; your eyes will see, and ears will hear

# November

## November 1

## No Odd Conversation

**Philippians 4:6**
*Be careful for nothing; but in every thing by prayer and supplication with thanksgiving let your requests be made known unto God.*

Prayer is like incense rising high from a trusting heart, soaring
Or, if coming from one without Joy or thankfulness, it is boring
Worry or worship; prayer will reflect what your mind is believing
Unless there's beauty and delight, it is hard to pray with meaning

Rejoice in prayer, sing, read, meditate, or keep a diary and record
I can see your heart and sense the Joy of authentic Faith in accord
Chat with me as your Faithful Friend; in conversation, don't be odd
Our heart-to-heart interaction of Love, acknowledging Me as Lord

## November 2

## Not for Storing

**Proverbs 11:25**
*The liberal soul shall be made fat: and he that watereth shall be watered also himself.*

Give generously and confidently as prosperous heirs of the King
I fill empty vessels, do not hoard fearing lack, give Me everything
Do not accumulate, building surplus; meet needs without worrying
You must use the wealth I provide for My work; it is not for storing

Count your blessings, and be grateful for My faithful, timely provision
Freely share with others because God has blessed you, in appreciation
Steward your wealth, great or small and be generous in your distribution
Let your witness touch all who cross your path, and tell of My Redemption

## November 3

## Self-Degradation

**1 John 3:22**
*And whatsoever we ask, we receive of him, because we keep his commandments, and do those things that are pleasing in his sight.*

There is no limit to My Supply; but often, you create the restriction
You block distributing channels when you hoard My divine provision
Or by submitting blasphemous, miserly requests for My consideration
I am longing to share My abundance; don't insult me by self-degradation

I have shared the secret of mountain-moving Faith; try it out sometime
Do not be content with penny-pinching poverty, but shift your paradigm
There is no limit to My Power; ask of Me, the nations I will give to mine
How I fulfill My promises is My business, yours only to trust, not whine

## November 4

## Emmanuel, God with You

**John 20:31**

*But these are written, that ye might believe that Jesus is the Christ, the Son of God; and that believing ye might have life through his name.*

Understand that you cannot obtain My fullness of Joy by human effort
Can you force a friend to spend time with you to receive his comfort?
No, it is your mutual understanding to be available anytime for support
Calling Me is not a summons; I Am Emmanuel, God with you, as escort

When you cry out My name Jesus, it will open your eyes to understand
The humbler you become, the nearer to Me you get to My loving hand
You experience the thrill of My Presence and realize your Savior I Am
And no matter what troubles you got into, I knew them all beforehand

End doublemindedness, blind-sided by the world, you fell into a snare
The humbler you become, the closer to Me you get, where no evil dare

Our relationship deepens; you turn away from sin and lose your despair
Just know that nothing can distance us, submit everything to My care

## November 5

## The Second Coming

**1 Thessalonians 4:16–17**

*For the Lord himself shall descend from heaven with a shout, with the voice of the archangel, and with the trump of God: and the dead In*
*Christ shall rise first: Then we which are alive and remain shall be caught up together with them in the clouds, to meet the Lord in the air:*
*and so shall we ever be with the Lord.*

My followers' wholehearted surrender to Me could change humankind
If only all who believe in Me as Lord and Christ united with one mind
I would liberate every human being, take back My world and mankind
My delayed Second Coming is because I want no one to be left behind

If My children lived for Me, My Return the sweetest music to their ears
Long ago, I would have redeemed My world and allayed all your fears
Boldly witness, declare Salvation is free in Me; I have dried your tears
Abandon futile desires, tell lost souls of My Love; time is short in years

## November 6

## My Power Is Yours

**John 15:5**

*I Am the Vine, ye are the branches: He that abideth in me, and I in him, the same bringeth forth much fruit: for without me ye can do nothing.*

*God in action* is what Power is; it is not something overwhelming
But men liken it to a great force when life is in crisis, like lightning
No, it is not; any servant of Mine has My Power in good standing
*All* you do is powerful if you live in Me, and together we are walking

Hold this thought when discouraged if your accomplishments are little
My Divine Spirit works in you; expel the self, let My keen axe whittle
You are My masterpiece, My work in progress, and I will never belittle
Trust Me; a sharp axe is of little value without My Master Hand in battle

Count no day wasted on which new spiritual insight you have gained
If you offered up the day for My use, you might wonder what I attained
Bearing fruit is My job; displaying it yours; I Am the true Vine ordained
I send life-giving sap to the branches; read the Scripture; it is explained

## November 7

## Self Is the One Block

**John 7:38**

*He that believeth on me, as the scripture hath said, out of his belly shall flow rivers of living water.*

Living in Me, loving My Will, you happily labor in My vineyard
As you become a channel for My Spirit and My worthy vanguard
Do not say you only add little value; it is the false pride of a coward
I send the water to give life; an unblocked pipe only passes it onward

Make sure you do nothing to stem the living water that I bestow
Self is the one block that impedes the stream: your pride swallow
Serve all who cross your path, faithfully channel My Love to flow
Remember, it is not by your might but by My Spirit that I restore

## November 8

## If You Don't Forgive

**Philippians 3:13**

*One thing I do, forgetting those things which are behind, and reaching forth unto those things which are before, I press toward the mark for the prize of the high calling of God in Christ Jesus.*

Do not carry the burdens of the past; keep only the best memories
Erase everything hurtful; forget every failure; retain only love stories
Bearing the deadweight of sin, you mock the victory that is Calvary's
If you don't forgive others, My load you grow and sorrows increase

## November 9

## Our Unique Partnership

**John 15:15**

*Henceforth I call you not servants; for the servant knoweth not what his*
*lord doeth: but I have called you friends; for all things that I have heard*
*of my Father I have made known unto you.*

I Am your best Friend, but do you realize the wonder of our Friendship?
You honor Me with Love, obedience, and understanding in your worship
But it cannot be one-way; think, what can I do for you in our relationship?
It becomes more meaningful when you know I consider this a partnership

I, too, need the assurance that I can count on you for your glad service
The harvest is ready; I need help; I'd like you to work as My apprentice
Our is a unique Friendship, for I give you a life purpose you cannot miss
Dwell often on the Joy of knowing your Creator and Redeemer like this

## November 10

## Failures I Shoulder

**1 John 5:4**

*For whatsoever is born of God overcometh the world: and this is the victory that overcometh the world, even our faith.*

Life's challenges and hardships are not obstacles to your progress
As new opportunities for faster growth, they only call for your best
You must come up with new moves as you do in the game of chess
Nothing can overcome you in My Presence, do not dwell on weakness

You are in a race you must complete, know I Am waiting at the finish
Whatever is daunting must be surmounted; let not your hopes diminish
Remember, it is not by might or power; it's by My Spirit you accomplish
I have equipped you with everything you need, together we will vanquish

Minor issues hidden away can become giants you will have to conquer
Anything swept under the carpet, you have to deal with sooner or later

You cannot fail if you are with Me, but My definition of success
does differ
Still, I will have you triumph in your journey to Me; any failures
I shoulder

## November 11

## You Are Mine

**Ephesians 2:10**

*For we are His workmanship, created in Christ Jesus unto good works,*
*which God hath before ordained that we should walk in them.*

Periodically, look back at your life, you will realize every step I planned
I chiseled each precious stone, as a perfect fit for the mosaic I designed
Try to imagine My thrill and longing for the masterpiece I predestined
Fearfully and wonderfully made, you are precious in My eyes and mine!

One thing you should know, I set My prized gemstones in Heaven's hues
No human eye can gaze at My finished work till life on earth discontinues
Until you are beyond the veil from this world of thrall into liberty's virtues
Into eternity, the shining jewel of the saved, where the mystery continues

## November 12

## My Thoughts You Occupy

**Job 7:11**
*Therefore I will not refrain my mouth; I will speak in the anguish of my spirit; I will complain in the bitterness of my soul.*

Heaven's music cannot drown your voiceless, anguished cry
It pierces My heart like no other sound, be certain I will reply
Theologians may complicate My Word, but your needs I supply
Be sure I hear every plea; in My thoughts, it is you who occupy

## November 13

## Seldom Visit?

**Ezekiel 11:16**
*Therefore say, Thus saith the Lord GOD; Although I have cast them far off among the heathen, and although I have scattered them among the countries, yet will I be to them as a little sanctuary in the countries where they shall come.*

Understand that My call, "Come to Me," is a loving invitation
Do not see it as your duty or debt to Me; that is not My intention
My Calling you has meaning that will surpass your imagination
For every fear, solving every problem, know I have the solution

Are your days dull and dreary? Does life feel as if it is all random?
Come to Me—whether it is a physical, mental, or spiritual problem
Have hope in Me; I Am your best Friend; we can journey in tandem
In a hostile world, I Am your Sanctuary; why are your visits seldom?

## November 14

## Man Traded Heaven

**Ecclesiastes 3:11**

*He hath made every thing beautiful in his time: also he hath set the world in their heart, so that no man can find out the work that God maketh from the beginning to the end.*

Man has made of Life what never was your heavenly Father's design
Before the Fall of Man, Paradise was God's Love and bounty benign
Enticing and defiling man, evil entered the world and began to reign
Cruelty took control; man has tasted pain and hardship since that time

How did the Fall occur long ago, and why was man so stupid not wise
So beautiful was God's creation, nature's bounty a delight to your eyes
The Maker's artistry in mountains, foliage, oceans, and cobalt-blue skies
For mere knowledge, man traded Heaven not much wiser for his exercise

## November 15

## An Encore

**2 Corinthians 4:15**
*For all things are for your sakes, that the abundant grace might through the thanksgiving of many redound to the glory of God.*

Do you believe in miracles or think that they do not happen anymore?
Make no mistake; your Faith, even as a mustard seed, I do not embargo
If you trust Me in choosing the day and the hour, I will do an encore
Manifest My miracle-working Power today and, if needed, tomorrow

It will be even as it was when I walked the earth with My Apostles
To heal, rescue and restore Life, I built their Faith with My miracles
They learned to trust Me, so must you and glorify Me in your troubles
Humility admits doubt, and I Am aware you must build Faith's muscles

Fear not; I know when to intervene; in your hour of need, do not despair
Believe in Me, and I will not ever let you down; I'll do something singular

Know the heart of your Miracle-working Savior, for you are in My care
Review the spectacular feats I performed on earth; do not stay unaware

## November 16

## Love and Unity

**Mark 12:30–31**
*And thou shalt love the Lord thy God with all thy heart, and with all*
*thy soul, and with all thy mind, and with all thy strength: this is the first*
*commandment. And the second is like, namely this, Thou shalt love thy*
*neighbour as thyself. There is none other commandment greater than these.*

When you gather in My name, lovers, friends, or neighbors, I Am there
That is My promise you should never forget, for it is the unity we share
Broken relationships tear My heart; but by living in harmony, you declare
You are united in My Spirit; listen to My Voice, My Will is your prayer

In God's great diversity, you are many, yet you must be one in Christ
Gird yourselves with God's compassion; love one another, for I insist
It is not a suggestion, but My commandment, from all disunion, desist
Keep the unity of My Spirit in humility and gentleness; you must persist

Truly learn to Love and forgive; that is a vital lesson in the unity of Faith

It is not an examination to fail when you stand before Me as magistrate

If you say you Love Me and do not care for another, that is illegitimate

Loving God and man is so simple but profound; it is My main mandate

## November 17

## Faithful Doorkeeper

**Matthew 25:2**
*Well done, thou good and faithful servant. Enter thou into the Joy of thy Lord.*

Who do you think I Am speaking to when these words I whisper?
Not the rich and famous or influential, but My humblest follower
Bravely facing every hardship cheerfully, My smiling cross bearer
Living in Truth and obedience, always My ever-faithful doorkeeper

It is a divine invitation for My children to enter the Joy of their Lord
The world never sees their steadfast, quiet service; I keep a record
Caring not for wealth or fame, they work to share My saving Word
For all you bold witnesses, I reserve My eternal Joy as your reward

That is the prize for unflinching duty, the Joy of the Lord's anointing
Divine Joy honoring your service and commending long-suffering
Whether you know it on earth or in Heaven, it is spiritually everlasting
Having no connection to earthly pleasures, this transcendent rejoicing

Incomparable and exclusive it is for My loved ones in all circumstances
Once received, it cannot be taken away by anyone or any disturbances
Do not fear adversity and hardship; they are opportunities, not injustices
Live cheerfully in My Kingdom, bringing Me your suffering and services

## November 18

## Reveal My Glory

**Colossians 1:27**

*To whom God would make known what is the riches of the glory of this mystery among the Gentiles; which is Christ in you, the hope of glory.*

The beauty of character is the Glory of your Lord and Savior
Yours too in new birth but on earth only partially in your power
God's blazing purity and Love are too brilliant for you to shoulder
But the Glory rises on you when your life mirrors it as My follower

The world must know our heavenly Father; reveal then My Glory
Tell of His holiness, compassion, and long-suffering in your story
Affirm how life changes when you realize God is so reconciliatory
Your sins, once forgiven, He remembers them no more in memory

## November 19

## Don't Be Shortsighted

**Isaiah 40:26**

*Lift up your eyes on high, and behold who hath created these things, that*
*bringeth out their host by number: he calleth them all by names by the*
*greatness of his might, for that he is strong in power; not one faileth.*

From where does your help come? Lift up your eyes, the Lord, to seek
Scorn the falsehood, gloom, and sleaze of the earth; it makes you weak
When you are vulnerable, look to the hills where help comes for the meek
For if you stay chained to the world, your future will always look bleak

Do not be shortsighted; focus on the long view, in life you need a vision
I Am the Lord of heaven and earth; you can count on My intervention
Nature knows My bounty, but you, the living waters of My Redemption
Which means no spiritual or material lack; completely trust My provision

## November 20

## Know Me, No Fear; No Me, Know Fear

**Psalm 51:6**
*Behold, thou desirest truth in the inward parts: and in the hidden part thou shalt make me to know wisdom.*

Be sure of a future content and joyful by living more and more in Me
You will have peace, no matter what; always forgive, you will stay free
Set your hope on things above, not on earthly things; that is My plea
Fear the Lord, gain My wisdom and grace, all who hope in My mercy

Mysteries of the spirit world are better left alone, do not investigate
There are secrets in My Word; search for My truths and disseminate
Go deeper into Me; I Am your Light and Life; there is no alternate
In Me are all the answers you need, here and in the hereafter state

Theology is knowing Me; not the scholarly knowledge that is obscure
Humble fishermen, I chose, not high priests, to spread My Scripture
I Am all you need to know about God; ignore the falsehood out there
Know Me, No Fear; No Me, Know Fear, it is a fact, not meant to scare

## November 21

## Triumph Not Gloom

**Isaiah 50:7**
*For the Lord GOD will help me; therefore shall I not be confounded: therefore have I set my face like a flint, and I know that I shall not be ashamed.*

Is your Faith and Joy in Me hidden away, or is it jubilant and contagious?
If you hide your candle under a bushel, men will not know; that is obvious
When set on a candlestick you make it known to all; it is not anonymous
It gives light to all in your path, men will have no doubt, they will be jealous

That is how your witness will be if it springs from trust, your life in Me
Being cheerlessly resigned to My Will reveals doubts and uncertainty
It does not reflect My abundant Life; My Love and Joy are a guarantee
Conquer with My guidance, trusting My Presence overcomes adversity

Remember the Hosannas in Jerusalem; I anticipated My death and scorn
My disciples and I came in triumph, not in gloom; neither did we mourn

At My Last Supper, I had instituted My New Covenant marking My sojourn
I set My face like flint to die on Rome's Cross so that men would be reborn

## November 22

## Only Love-Inspired Significance

**John 13:34–35**

*A new commandment I give unto you, That ye love one another; as I*
*have loved you, that ye also love one another. By this shall all men know that ye are my disciples, if ye have love one to another.*

God is Love; no ifs, ands or buts, it is your Heavenly Father's character
It naturally follows that only what is motivated by Love can last forever
I simplified the Great Commandment; Love God and Love your neighbor
Love is the benchmark for your work for me; consider it My Magna Carta

Love is the essence of God; without it, the world's accolades are useless
Fame and applause coming your way does not always mean real progress
Even if you speak with the tongues of men and angels, it may be aimless
Only what gets done in Love counts and endures, and that is true success

Have you seen how only a smile, or a kind word makes such a difference?
That is part of God's design; no matter how simple it seems, it is evidence

Whereas the greatest knowledge is worthless if it denies God's existence
For the test of all that is pure and perfect is its Love-inspired significance

Eliminate everything in your heart and life that is loveless, and bear fruit
Much of what people do is in vain because pride is their primary pursuit
So many do work in My Name, which I do not acknowledge but refute
When you do not Love one another, for My Word, you do not give a hoot

## November 23

## No Exception

**John 16:33**

*These things I have spoken unto you, that in me ye might have peace.*
*In the world ye shall have tribulation: but be of good cheer; I have overcome the world.*

If I have overcome the world, why do My children face tribulation?
I said discipleship is self-denial and carrying a Cross, no exception
No one can ever accuse Me of securing allegiance with deception
Count the cost, lest you turn back because suffering is a condition

I warned you would get hated like sheep and by wolves devoured
Arrested and scourged before governors and kings under their rod
Even your loved ones would persecute you and have you outlawed
Whoever kills you will think that his service is an offering to God

Faced with this reality, many went back and walked with Me no more
It is the choice of My true disciples; will you suffer for your Faith or go?

My children, who learned the secret of contentment and Joy, stand sure
Suffering more than the prosperous and proud, yet it is Me they adore

Theirs is a supernatural power not available to those who do not believe
Ready to dredge the cup of trial and misfortune, scorning what many achieve
With every reason to complain, for losing pleasures to which people cleave
Rejoicing in tribulation because they are sure of eternity's privileges to receive

My overcoming was never for Myself but for you, My beloved children
My followers saw a lost cause when the chief priests had Me stricken
Reviled, spat upon, scourged, they deemed Me conquered, forbidden
Only My Father could discern My unflinching Spirit though I was smitten

I showed God to man, but you needed to see your God, the all-powerful
Unconquered, unharmed, untouched by evil and its power; He is Faithful
In Me is the promise of victory; I have overcome the world; I Am Truthful
Learn from My Resurrection that I Am above earth's ways, it is all vengeful

Take heart from My victory, be glad for your trials even if you get ravaged

Know you must share in My tribulations for evil to leave you unchallenged
Be of good cheer; you are on My side; hence the evil onslaught deranged
Rest in My Peace and conquering Power, be sure you will not get damaged

## November 24

## Sacrifice Rewarded

**Romans 12:1**

*I beseech you therefore, brethren, by the mercies of God, that ye present*
*your bodies a living sacrifice, holy, acceptable unto God, which is your*
*reasonable service.*

Whatever happens in the day, consider it is work you are doing for Me
That is the way to usher in My blessings on everything, My guarantee
My mission and your life work become the same; we are a committee
Together we will save My world; offer your best to Me as My devotee

God's message of hope we must communicate till it is time to terminate
How much longer His plans prolong, My Father knows; there is no debate
My children, your faithfulness is required; it is a sacrifice, and I appreciate
I call you to live in two worlds; to deny the one you know is My mandate

I know it is not easy and often beyond the power of your understanding
How challenging it is; to overcome your flesh and to keep on opposing

Only trust that sacrificing your life for Me is redemptive and rewarding
It's almost harvest time; the fields are getting ready; the hour is coming

## November 25

## Your Servant King

**Colossians 3:12–13**

*Put on therefore, as the elect of God, holy and beloved, bowels of mercies,*
*kindness, humbleness of mind, meekness, long suffering; Forbearing one*
*another, and forgiving one another.*

What do you see in Me, the Owner of all creation, pride or humility?
Why does the Maker of Heaven and earth manifest degrading docility?
Knocking on doors of unbelieving hearts when turned away in hostility?
Scorned by many who mock and sneer yet continue to plead in futility?

"Behold, I stand at the door and knock," offering My humble invitation
Even to those who feel no need for Me; I plead to bridge our separation
Behind rudely barred doors, I know that some souls need My restoration
I Am your Servant King, knocking and never giving up on reconciliation

Learn from Me that humility is the key to life, pride rules in the jungle
Men may believe that they are wise, but in My eyes, it is contemptible

If you lift yourself on high, you deny God's Word, and you will
stumble
Haughty looks, proud hearts, I oppose but I love the meek and
humble

I will never use the proud but judge with My rod those who are
obstinate
You will meet people who may shut you out, but you are not to
retaliate
Riches and wealth are mine, but I became poor; your sins to
exonerate
Remember, I Am your example; consider how I'd react and
communicate

Be alert to your Savior's concern for man's happiness, give of
your best
Dwell on My Word and emulate My great humility; it is true
Love's test
Treasure My Peace, it is My plea "Come to Me, and I will give
you rest"
A tranquility you cannot find in the world is yours, even in the
tempest

## November 26

## Find Your Treasure

**Isaiah 53:2**

*For he shall grow up before him as a tender plant, and as a root out of a dry ground: he hath no form nor comeliness; and when we shall*
*see him, there is no beauty that we should desire him.*

Born in human flesh, I chose a body with no allure for men to adore
The long-awaited Messiah men did not recognize but came to abhor
My close followers knew the grace and beauty of My Spirit for sure
They discerned My character; you, too, know Me; find your treasure

Let not the world distort your understanding of My mysteries henceforth
It is Love that rules all My interactions; I created you; I know your worth
The hearing ear, and the seeing eye, I made them; pray you will have both
And Faith to see the grace and beauty of the Godhead for spiritual growth

## November 27

## I Never Thwart

**Ephesians 5:17**
*Wherefore be ye not unwise, but understanding what the will of the Lord is.*

Many people think that submission of their will is My harsh command
To submit your free will resentfully is something I would never demand
In desiring and loving My Will, your happiness and Spirit-rest will expand
In doubt, pray not to surrender to My Will but to know Me and understand

Grow to Love Me, and there will come a certainty that serves you best
And that is what I want for you and your loved ones, only the choicest
How could anyone imagine that thwarting My children is ever My interest
Little do you know I long to grant your prayers, help you in your conquest

## November 28

## From My Spirit Within

**Ephesians 1:13**
*In whom ye also trusted, after that ye heard the word of truth, the gospel of your salvation: in whom also after that ye believed, ye were sealed with that holy Spirit of promise.*

I call you, My friends, rest in My Word for your eternal salvation
Let your Joy in our Friendship fill you, build life's very foundation
Sharpen your mind, focus on My Presence; we are now in a union
Our work and interests merge; we share a purpose and cooperation

Big ambitions and a desire for worldly fame, I do not recommend
I cutaway your ties binding you to cravings on which you depend
Creating a firm footing for our Friendship, one that will never end
Your inner life in Me must deepen before venturing out to ascend

It is the way of My Spirit, a change of heart, strength from within
Obedience to what the Scriptures say and turning away from sin
You set affections on things above, for God's Will is your linchpin
Loving others as I have loved you, in humility and with a thick skin

## November 29

## Agree in My Name

**Matthew 18:19–20**
*Again I say unto you, That if two of you shall agree on earth as touching any thing that they shall ask, it shall be done for them of my Father which is in heaven. For where two or three are gathered together in my name, there am I in the midst of them.*

Weigh My Words; every one counts; every promise you can pursue
If two or three meet in My Name, seek My Will; surely, I Am with you
Your self-invited companion, one with you, granting all petitions true
For in unity, your demands are mine, if we share the same worldview

Study the Scriptures carefully; the context for these words of Mine
It is more than asking and getting, it's a conflict resolution guideline
Gently dealing with brothers and sisters in error who need discipline
Using agreement and consensus, with Me in your midst to determine

## November 30

## Your Sanctuary

**Exodus 15:17**
*Thou shalt bring them in, and plant them in the mountain of thine inheritance, in the place, O LORD, which thou hast made for thee to dwell in, in the Sanctuary, O Lord, which thy hands have established.*

There are times you want to get away when you need Sanctuary
You need time for yourself, to retreat from others for quiet reverie
Tired of being misunderstood for you are criticized even by family
To escape from failure, sins, or shortcomings, where can you flee?

To Me, your hiding place, to your Creator, the only One you need
In My immensity, forget all your troubles; My Peace is guaranteed
Abide in Me, know the relief and Joy of My refuge, to Me concede
Eternal Sanctuary is in My Love; from all your fears, you are freed

# December

## December 1

## The Bread of Life

**Luke 19:41–42**

*And when he was come near, he beheld the city, and wept over it, Saying, If thou hadst known, even thou, at least in this thy day, the things which belong unto thy peace! but now they are hid from thine eyes.*

I understand your failings; know I Am a genuinely human Jesus
Hardships and victories I see, your failures too, even if serious
While on earth, I was more often with sinners than the virtuous
My disciples saw My heart for hungry multitudes was generous

But I had to teach them lessons to recognize Divine Parenthood
To learn that sympathy without responsibility achieves no good
They had suggested a starved, exhausted crowd go and find food
Five loaves and two fish to feed five thousand. Few understood

Stomachs fill up for a while; appetites demand more if not sated
The mob wanted more without discerning the One who delighted
The Jews did not remember the words that Moses had predicted
That God would be sending One to care for the poor and afflicted

Pity, without a remedy for evil or need, can bring no transformation
I Am the Bread of Life; the Galileans wanted mere carnal satisfaction

My Presence is your Peace; let it not be hidden from your perception

Prophets had foretold, but Jerusalem forgot the time of My Visitation

## December 2

## Do Not Surrender

**1 Timothy 6:12**
*Fight the good fight of faith, lay hold on eternal life, where unto thou*
*art also called, and hast professed a good profession before many witnesses.*

Take off your shoes as Moses did at the burning bush in adoration
Worship Me with reverence, for I Am God, worthy of your devotion
I call you, My friends; grow in Faith knowing My Majesty and position
Your intimacy with the Son of God is the miracle of our divine union

Draw close to Me, you can demand, for insistent prayer is no crime
Your God is a consuming fire, but confidence in worship is sublime
Ask but also listen; your God is your Brother too, a mystery divine
I long for you to be true to your Life's mission in service to mankind

There is a Calling for every man and woman, but so many blunder
You are discouraged if people let you down, but I Am their Mentor

My disappointment is real for My children; their defeats I shoulder
Keep this in mind, fight the good fight, in troubles do not surrender

## December 3

## Grand Adventure

**Psalm 23:4**

*Yea, though I walk through the valley of the shadow of death, I will fear no evil: for thou art with me; thy rod and thy staff they comfort me.*

I did not design you to figure out every situation you face in life
Answers may hide in eternity; all is not butter cut easily by a knife
Fretting needlessly about things you cannot solve only adds to strife
A few setbacks on a journey are fine if nice surprises too are rife

Only make sure you invite Me, then life can be a grand adventure
Companions, we will tackle challenges together at every juncture
My Presence will make your travel meaningful, with less pressure
Facing hardships with My Joy because I Am with you in the picture

## December 4

## Live It; Don't Debate

**Isaiah 53:3**

*He is despised and rejected of men; a man of sorrows, and acquainted with grief: and we hid as it were our faces from him; he was despised,*
*and we esteemed him not.*

Isaiah prophesied I would be despised and rejected, a Man of Sorrows
You love Me or, like many, scorn the One who cares for your tomorrows
Compare Heaven's values against the world, the resemblance narrows
Men esteem prestige: the lowly Son of God got rejected like Quasimodo

The mob that shouted Hosanna forced their verdict on Pilate to dictate
Care not for the world's values; only My Kingdom code must motivate
Seek not men's applause; as My witness, you too will encounter hate
People do not give a hoot for the Truth if you don't live it to only debate

Amid that screaming horde, do not miss God's Majesty in My Presence
I could have stopped the crowd from judicial murder without evidence

Man's acclaim would have ended Redemption had I traded My sentence
I chose a crown of thorns and the Cross to save your eternal inheritance

Trying times will come for you, too; stay close when you get discouraged
Yours is the cause of Truth; rely on Me, not men, no matter how privileged
Men will fail you, too, causing hardship and grief; remember, I got ravaged
I Am always beside you in suffering and sorrow; fear not, be encouraged

## December 5

## Be Great Givers

**Luke 6:38**
*Give, and it shall be given unto you; good measure, pressed down, and shaken together, and running over, shall men give into your bosom. For with the same measure that ye mete withal it shall be measured to you again.*

Make habitual giving a spiritual pursuit, scorn earthly treasure
Every life that crosses yours give generously; do not measure
Share love, understand, and pray for all in need, do not lecture
Blessed with money and goods, provide cheerfully and nurture

Learn to be great givers, for your heavenly Father is not a miser
On the evil and the good, He pours out His blessings and favor
He sends rain to all, the just and the unjust; His ways are higher
God alone is your standard; fear no lack when He is your Provider

Give boldly according to need, not timidly keeping dearth in mind
You know your Father in Heaven; the Great Giver never falls behind
Imitate Him and give lavishly, consider the urgency, to bias be blind
As I supply your needs, you, too, serve all whom I guide you to find

## December 6

## Spiritual Warfare

**James 1:12**

*Blessed [is] the man that endureth temptation: for when he is tried, he*
*shall receive the crown of life, which the Lord hath promised to them*
*that love him.*

As soon as you sense the enticement, disengage from the temptation
It can be anything to make you disobey Me and try to disrupt our union
The first step to conquer is to summon God's Word, for immediate action
In tiredness, illness, poverty, stress, or depression, do not yield to Satan

Committed to My Great Commission, you will engage in spiritual warfare
Forces of evil will constantly assail your defenses, and you must beware
Every onslaught of the beasts of Hell will seek to defeat you and ensnare
I have called you to spread the Good News of My salvation; are you aware?

Draw souls to Me, and let nothing prevent you from fulfilling your mission
You are not a passive victim; choose to sin or overcome life's temptation

Confess your failings to Me in repentance and Faith; seek transformation
For the love of Me, fight the good fight; do not yield to carnal inclination

## December 7

## Your Life Source

**Ephesians 6:6**

*Not with eye service, as men-pleasers; but as the servants of Christ, doing the will of God from the heart.*

My disciples struggled to learn; your spiritual journey is no different
There is a principle that is true in nature and the spiritual environment
The Law of the Center in the sublime union with God works to cement
And the soul discerns reliable sustenance comes from divine attachment

The Will of God is your life source; food can sustain only the physical
A soul that disregards the Bread of Life scorns Power that is spiritual
Your meat is to do My Will; I will nourish, do not focus on the biological
I Am your Center; delight in My Will and turn as I lead, that, is critical

## December 8

## The Kingdom of God

**Luke 19:11**

*And as they heard these things, he added and spake a parable, because he was nigh to Jerusalem, and because they thought that the kingdom of God should immediately appear.*

Mine was a lost cause on earth; even My disciples half believed
They fled for their lives, shocked My Mission I had not achieved
Even at the Cross, some expected a miracle from Me to succeed
Despite My teaching, a worldly kingdom is what they had perceived

Yes, My teaching touched their hearts; they knew I was powerful
But they anticipated a military call to action that would be forceful
When sentenced like a criminal, My fate to them seemed so pitiful
I washed their feet at the Last Supper, and they were still doubtful

A spiritual Kingdom I taught; they thought the world was stronger
Doubting Thomas revealed I Am God, not just another messenger
My Resurrection presented proof; their Hope and Faith triggered
Then they remembered all I had taught and no longer felt cornered

Trusting their Messiah, assured of My Divinity, they became fearless

Holy Spirit empowered for My work on earth, they started to witness
Safe in My realm, they preached the Kingdom of God, their business
Their wondrous works greater than mine in lives saved with success

Strong in My Spirit, they boldly spread the Good News of salvation
Sharing God's love for all humanity, His gift, peace of mind in union
Forgiveness of sin and eternal life, giving evidence in their deposition
That Gospel Truth makes even a fool wise in spiritual transformation

## December 9

## Seek to Save

**Matthew 5:16**

*Let your light so shine before men, that they may see your good works, and glorify your Father which is in heaven.*

All seek Me, but few know what they want and remain dissatisfied
They do not recognize I Am the object of their longing, the true Guide
If only men realized, My Life, Death and Resurrection are unqualified
Count it your greatest Joy: to reveal why I was born, lived, and died

Life anew three-hundred sixty-five days with God is a guarantee
Humanity's quest can end if, in your heart and soul, they see Me
Profit, despite hardship, trials, and challenges, if I Am their trustee
If communion with My Father was vital for Me, it is not idle curiosity

Mobs will not rush into My Kingdom; it is only the still, small voice
That can persuade men to listen and help them decide on their choice
The hateful multitude does not care for the Son of God's sacrifice
It has no desire for quiet prayer nor to follow Me in stony prejudice

## December 10

## Understanding Silence

**Psalm 50:3**
*Our God shall come, and shall not keep silence: a fire shall devour before*
*him, and it shall be very tempestuous round about him.*

I most often communicate with you inaudibly, wordlessly and in silence
It is unlikely I will instruct directly; more often, you will feel the distance
The Way leading to Life is narrow, not wide, but few know the difference
As you learn more of Me, in our quiet times, you will sense My Presence

Amid life's burdens and clamor, silently reflect, meditate, and persevere
I Am with you though we do not speak, sit quietly, do not rush; I Am there
Wait on Me; read if you like or pray; formality is unnecessary in My sphere
I connect without speaking; in My comfort and Peace, you lose all your fear

Friends understand love expressed in many ways, often incommunicado
When I Am silent in your troubles; you wonder why, and you want to know

I have given you all you need to overcome, and tough times
help you grow
Know I need you, too; sometimes, your understanding I ask you
to show

## December 11

## For Your Endurance

**Isaiah 43:19**

*Behold, I will do a new thing; now it shall spring forth; shall ye not know it?*
*I will even make a way in the wilderness and rivers in the desert.*

Has your life been full of struggle and care? Has living been miserable?
Know you have experienced the agony of My poor world in My crucible
In Faith, did you sacrifice your life for Me, making yourself expendable?
To you, My Peace and Joy, for you are precious in My sight, unshakable

Watch, I make all things new; for your endurance, obtain a second spring
Your heart, I will gladden and fill every dawn with My Spirit's indwelling
My loving care will enable each day's duties; there will be no foreboding
I will fulfill your hopes with My steadfast love, your aspirations surpassing

## December 12

## Two Different Fears

**Genesis 15:1**

*After these things the word of the Lord came unto Abraham in a vision, saying, Fear not, Abram: I Am thy shield, and thy exceeding great reward.*

It is essential you understand that fear and love cannot intermingle
Godly fear that leads you to wisdom is different from the fear of evil
Evil seeks to terrify; God's perfect love cancels the fear of the devil
That fear overrules feeble, uncertain love, it is a dark force, terrible

My perfect love is a conquering force; it will defeat fear when you sin
On the Cross, I bore sin to gift you My divine righteousness, within
Do you believe I would want you to live in the terror of sin ever again?
Past, Present, Future sins repented; I do not remember; I have forgiven

I Am sinless, you continue to fight sin, your new life My transformation
I Am Love, the Father and I are one; you live fearless in our perfection
Do not use your privilege as a license to sin but live a holy life in action

Show Me initiative to overcome sin, as you experience My confirmation

At Calvary, I did everything for your new life to begin; I do not interfere
In man's free will uninvited, but to survive sin, you surely need a Savior
The wages of sin is death; I trampled death by death, made you My heir
I redeemed you to make you holy; believe in Me, and be of good cheer

Every fear gets banished only by My Presence and the Power of My Name
Fear the future? You have dread only if you ignore Me for wealth or fame
Fear of poverty? Seek My Kingdom first, and all your needs you can claim
The temptations of fear are many; cast them aside; for you are not the same

## December 13

## Your Forever Guide

**Ephesians 6:11**
*Put on the whole armour of God, that ye may be able to stand against the wiles of the devil.*

I Am your forever Guide; rest assured, you are safe in My care
Know that I have your back; have Joy in Me, for none can dare
I planned your life to a tee, My love for you is beyond compare
But do not rush ahead of Me; troubles ensue, evil forces ensnare

Be patient, always yield to My Spirit and the Power of My Word
Life is a battlefield; proceed as I guide, do not follow the herd
The charge to see you through is mine; nothing is disordered
Worry denies My guidance; your fears can leave Me bewildered!

## December 14

## Stand Relentless

**Proverbs 10:25**
*As the whirlwind passeth, so is the wicked no more: but the righteous*
*is an everlasting foundation.*

Tempests and storms in nature proclaim the majesty of My creation
They roar in life, too, impotent to batter souls under My protection
No miracle can compare with the rebirth of a soul in transformation
The powers of evil rage, try to lay siege, but they end in humiliation

We walk together in the cool of a garden amidst all of life's uproar
It does not matter, life in a rowdy metropolis or the quiet seashore
Live in Me, in a Peace that passes all understanding, forevermore
There will be blizzards, tornadoes, and hurricanes; In all, I restore

An army will not storm the empty desert; it will assail the fortress
Expect onslaughts in your journey; you will draw forces of darkness
When evil tries to destroy you remember you are not defenseless
All work for Me to save souls is fiercely opposed; stand relentless

## December 15

## Ever Present

**Psalm 68:3**

*But let the righteous be glad; let them rejoice before God: yea, let them*
*exceedingly rejoice.*

My Joy is a life-lasting adventure, not just a thrill or a mere sensation
Live daily in My Power and Presence; do not always want exhilaration
When life casts a shadow, I have not left you; that is not the explanation
It could be Me shading you from your enemies, ensuring your protection

Don't you have times of sweet fellowship in silence with your dearest?
Being together, if you do not converse, you don't doubt their closeness
There are days when duty calls and times of discussing shared interests
Be ever joyful in My Presence; know I consider your every prayer request

## December 16

## What Joy Is

**Psalm 126:5**
*They that sow in tears shall reap in Joy.*

Life is like a journey, and your current phase may be demanding
Forge ahead, and take it in your stride cheerfully; keep on walking
Weeping may endure for a night, but Joy will come in the morning
That is My reward but focus on your trek; do not lose your bearing

Devastated by their loss of hope, the disciples surrendered My Joy
Their acceptance of failure and defeat made Satan eager to destroy
Believing all was lost, they thought life and work had to redeploy
Seeing My empty tomb, their Faith and courage rebounded to enjoy

Your failures try to convince you that I will deny you My Presence
Recall I gently restored Peter and My disciples; study the evidence
Trust Me, when blinded by defeat, My Joy is the reward of patience
Be steadfast and brave, despite failings; for My love is your balance

## December 17

## Invitation Not Condition

**Psalm 89:26**

*He shall cry unto me, Thou art my Father, my God, and the rock of my*
*salvation.*

Delight in your special privileges, My children; you abide in My Kingdom
My Father showers earthly blessings on all, rain, and sunshine at random
But those who believe in God are different from those who prefer Sodom
Temporal blessings everyone obtains, but many deny My spiritual freedom

The blessings of My Kingdom I long to bestow on all without restriction
I came to save the world, not to condemn, and there is no disqualification
God feeds the just and the unjust, but My Kingdom demands perfection
Be ye perfect even as your Father in Heaven is perfect; it is My invitation

How can you be perfect, you wonder? Sin is impossible to sideline
The answer is you cannot; you can only exchange your life for mine
You cannot strive after Faith, only rest in your Faithful Lord, divine

My salvation, the only entrance to My Kingdom is God's gift, genuine

The call to perfection is not a standard man can meet in his sinful bent
Why the Lamb of God, who takes away the sins of the world, was sent
Though My Father is generous to all, this is the secret spiritual element
Imitate Him, bless and love and forgive everyone without any judgment

## December 18

## Do Greater Things

**John 14:12**
*Verily, verily, I say unto you, He that believeth on me, the works that I do shall he do also; and greater works than these shall he do; because I go unto my Father.*

Citizens of My Kingdom possess the key to My storehouse of delight
Treasures that the eye has not seen, nor the ear heard; all are your right
Claim My gifts eagerly; I wait to see you employ them all in My sight
Be zealous of your spiritual resources; bring many souls into My light

This magnificent earth I created with only a thought of My divine mind
I said you would do greater things and save more lives than in My time
So, ponder over an idea that could make a difference if spiritually mined
Make your heart a Bethany home where needy souls seek Me and find

## December 19

## My Forever Love

**Isaiah 41:13**
*For I the Lord thy God will hold thy right hand, saying unto thee, Fear not; I*
*will help thee.*

Fear nobody, nothing, not fear of poverty, sickness, future, or failure
I will never leave you, be sure of My Perfect Love; I Am always near
Cast out worry and dread, seek My perfection, and you are secure
Bring Me everything that is of concern; in My Presence, make it clear

Though I Am back in My glory, you are My own, foremost on My mind
I have not abandoned you to your fears; never think I left you behind
Remain constantly sure of My Presence; evil is alert and seeks to find
Something to jolt you with the dread to which you are easily inclined

Whatever it may be, some issue big or small, it provides evil an entrance
Before you know it, you succumb to sin, worry, and doubt in compliance

Instead, pray and bring Me all your needs, with thankfulness in evidence

Remember, My forever Love and Peace; they are your eternal inheritance

## December 20

## Conquer Fear

**Psalm 27:3**
*Though an host should encamp against me, my heart shall not fear: though war should rise against me, in this will I be confident.*

I have not given you a spirit of fear; fight it with all your might
Attack it as you would a contagion as soon as it comes in sight
For it seeks to rend My Love for you bit by bit, this cursed blight
Go to war against every little fear; crush each attempt outright

If you allow minor misgivings to pierce your heart and penetrate
They will chip away at your resolve; doubts grow and accumulate
Diminishing your Faith and trust in My Love, they try to truncate
Conquer your anxieties and depression and trust Me to checkmate

## December 21

## No Unknowns

**Psalm 46:10**

*Be still, and know that I am God: I will be exalted among the heathen, I will be exalted in the earth.*

My child, I am the Master of the universe and your daily ups and downs
Be sure every moment of your life I planned and ordered, no unknowns
Alert to My still, small voice, yield to directions telling you to slow down
Gently I lead, watch My cues, walk, do not run, and you will not breakdown

The snowdrop, the mighty oak, time, and the tide, they are My creation
I know what needs My tender touch and what can manage more tension
Amiably let Me know if you have a situation that needs My intervention
Remember, when friends have their way, you do not cut communication

## December 22

## Don't Be Bothered

**Psalm 138:7**
*Though I walk in the midst of trouble, thou wilt revive me: thou shalt*
*stretch forth thine hand against the wrath of mine enemies, and thy right*
*hand shall save me.*

My death and Resurrection made evil impotent, but it gets empowered
By those who refuse My protection, but have no fear, I have conquered
He who is in you is greater than the evil world's ruler; do not be bothered
Call on My Name when darkness tries to overcome; never get cornered

Manage every issue, big or small, confident of My Power and Protection
Train in the awareness of My Presence; the Tempter can create division
In Me, all fear of darkness ends with unshakable Faith in My Redemption
You will plow right through life's challenges by trusting in My direction

## December 23

### Two Different Views

**Matthew 10:34**

*Think not that I Am come to send peace on earth: I came not to send*
*peace, but a sword.*

My Peace passes all understanding; it is not the world's view of harmony
Journey with Me to share My Love, not any carnal sentiment that is phony
Make no accord with forces of darkness; turn away from their sanctimony
All is not in unison; the sword of the Prince of Peace is at war with tyranny

## December 24

## The First Coming

**John 1:14**
*And the Word was made flesh, and dwelt among us, (and we beheld his glory, the glory as of the only begotten of the Father,) full of grace*
*and truth.*

Remember, the Magi from the East, guided by the Christmas star
Did they expect to be humbled, to worship at a stable as an altar?
Or to meet Me, not as King and Lord, but as a babe in a manger?
With gold, frankincense, and myrrh, they worshipped their Maker

Along with the shepherds who heard the glad tidings, they learned
To worship in humility, for the God of glory was revealed in a shed
Gifts aren't required; genuine penitence is, My salvation I completed
For I came to redeem sinners not as their ruler but as a servant fated

## December 25

## The Best Gifts

**Matthew 2:11**

*[T]hey saw the young child with Mary his mother, and fell down, and*
*worshipped him: and when they had opened their treasures, they presented unto him gifts; gold, and frankincense, and myrrh.*

Follow Me in Humility, Service, Worship, Sacrifice, and Sanctification
Discern why meek and lowly hearts can enter the Kingdom of Heaven
If you do have some gifts to bring, they must meet My *Gold* specification
*Frankincense*—a life that is consecrated; *Myrrh*—to share My Crucifixion

## December 26

## Do Not Hoard

**Proverbs 21:21**

*He that followeth after righteousness and mercy findeth life, righteousness, and honour.*

If you truly trust Me, you will not pursue wealth to hoard with pride
Instead, seek righteousness and mercy, and rely on Me to provide
My supply is sufficient for your needs and work if in Me you abide
Let the world chase after money; it is not for you; I Am your Guide

Life can be a struggle at times with the fear of not having enough
The journey takes you through valleys and over hills, and it's rough
Consider My Will paramount let nothing else drive you and handcuff
Wealth accumulation is bondage; keep what you use, no extra stuff

Fear not, do not hoard for the future; it clearly shows your mistrust
A pilgrim is not a resident; forget all qualms; your motives readjust
There is work to be done, and time is short so be faithful and trust
Gold, silver, precious stones are to build your foundation, not to lust

## December 27

## Your Calling

**Matthew 7:14**

*Because strait is the gate, and narrow is the way, which leadeth unto life, and few there be that find it.*

When you get stripped of surplus in life, consider it a blessing
Placed on a firm foundation, know this is all part of My training
On the cornerstone you stand, Christ the Rock, is your Calling
Secure in Me, more confident every day in faithful undertaking

Gladly take the pathway that I show, ever mindful of your service
Scorning worldly dreams and fancies and exempt from all avarice
Joyful fulfillment with discipline as My miracle-working apprentice
Love and laugh till your work on earth gets done under My aegis

## December 28

## Sure of My Presence

**Philippians 4:5**
*Let your moderation be known unto all men. The Lord is at hand.*

You want to feel My nearness instead of being sure of My Presence
Wanting taste and touch is like asking for a sign demanding evidence
No proof do I give but of Jonah; My three days in the grave absence
To unbelievers, veiled from sight; to you, My Resurrection inheritance

Your conviction about Me, your risen Lord, matters, not mere feelings
Moods are fleeting; they come and go; circumstances keep changing
I keep My promises unaffected by situations, for My Grace is amazing
Do not ever doubt My Presence; I Am always near; receive My blessing

## December 29

## You and I Work

**Exodus 36:2**

*And Moses called Bezaleel and Aholiab, and every wise hearted man,*
*in whose heart the LORD had put wisdom, even every one whose heart*
*stirred him up to come unto the work to do it.*

Combine your work with prayer, and know I labor right beside you
Your success will come from the certainty I Am with you, that it is true
In Me, you live and move and have your being; press ahead, pursue
I will never forsake you; what men find impossible, you and I can do

## December 30

## Heed My Call

**John 10:10**
*The thief cometh not, but for to steal, and to kill, and to destroy: I am come that they might have life, and that they might have it more*
*abundantly.*

In this world of suffering and misery, do you understand My pain?
I wept for hard hearts in Jerusalem, and I grieve for all who disdain
My abundant Life, trying to survive evil in its relentless, cruel domain
In all, you undertake, seek to bring lost souls to Me, and I will sustain

I Am the Man of sorrows, rejected and despised, unloved, unwanted
When men do not come to obtain My joy-filled life, I Am devastated
I come to My own, and My own receive Me not; they are disinterested
It is time for the Great Harvest; heed My Call, labor, and get connected

## December 31

## Jesus the Conqueror

**Matthew 1:21**

*And she shall bring forth a son, and thou shalt call his name JESUS:*
*for he shall save his people from their sins. I will say of the LORD, He*
*is my refuge and my fortress: my God; in him will I trust.*

In My Name, Jesus, conquer; call on Me, Jesus, your friend and Savior
Come to Me not to beseech but in confident expectation as My partner
I Am Alpha and Omega, for the lost I came; My Name means Redeemer
Signifying eternal salvation for My people, the gift of our heavenly Father

I will set you free from all that afflicts you, not only vice and perversion
Worry, doubt, dread, anger, despair, irritation, lack of love and tension
All these are sins, too; rebirth in Me is your freedom and transformation
Use the Power of My Name to soar above troubles and petty disposition

I Am the Messiah, the Lord Christ, the Anointed One, at Calvary, crucified
I deliver from fear, adversity, failure, and scarcity; the humble are fortified

In the Power of the Name above all names, Jesus, the Lamb, prophesied
Your Defender, Captain and Shepherd, in My care, follow Me, be satisfied

# CHRISTIAN FAITH

Circle Books explores a wide range of disciplines within the field of Christian faith and practice. It also draws on personal testimony and new ways of finding and expressing God's presence in the world today.

If you have enjoyed this book, why not tell other readers by posting a review on your preferred book site. Recent bestsellers from Circle Books are:

**I Am With You** (Paperback)

John Woolley

These words of divine encouragement were given to John Woolley in his work as a hospital chaplain, and have since inspired and uplifted tens of thousands, even changed their lives.

Paperback: 978-1-90381-699-8 ebook: 978-1-78099-485-7

**God Calling**

A. J. Russell

365 messages of encouragement channelled from Christ to two anonymous "Listeners".

Hardcover: 978-1-905047-42-0 ebook: 978-1-78099-486-4

**The Long Road to Heaven,**
A Lent Course Based on the Film
Tim Heaton
This second Lent resource from the author of *The Naturalist and the Christ* explores Christian understandings of "salvation" in a five-part study based on the film *The Way*.
Paperback: 978-1-78279-274-1 ebook: 978-1-78279-273-4

**Abide In My Love**
More Divine Help for Today's Needs
John Woolley
The companion to *I Am With You, Abide In My Love* offers words of divine encouragement.
Paperback: 978-1-84694-276-1

**From the Bottom of the Pond**
The Forgotten Art of Experiencing God in the Depths of the Present Moment
Simon Small
*From the Bottom of the Pond* takes us into the depths of the present moment, to the only place where God can be found.
Paperback: 978-1-84694-066-8 ebook: 978-1-78099-207-5

**God Is A Symbol Of Something True**
Why You Don't Have to Choose Either a Literal Creator God or a Blind, Indifferent Universe
Jack Call
In this examination of modern spiritual dilemmas, Call offers the explanation that some of the most important elements of life are beyond our control: everything is fundamentally alright.
Paperback: 978-1-84694-244-0

**The Scarlet Cord**

Conversations With God's Chosen Women

Lindsay Hardin Freeman, Karen N. Canton

Voiceless wax figures no longer, twelve biblical women, outspoken, independent, faithful, selfless risk-takers, come to life in *The Scarlet Cord*.

Paperback: 978-1-84694-375-1

**Will You Join in Our Crusade?**

The Invitation of the Gospels Unlocked by the Inspiration of *Les Miserables*

Steve Mann

*Les Miserables'* narrative is entwined with Bible study in this book of 42 daily readings from the Gospels, perfect for Lent or anytime.

Paperback: 978-1-78279-384-7 ebook: 978-1-78279-383-0

**A Quiet Mind**

Uniting Body, Mind and Emotions in Christian Spirituality

Eva McIntyre

A practical guide to finding peace in the present moment that will change your life, heal your wounds and bring you a quiet mind.

Paperback: 978-1-84694-507-6 ebook: 978-1-78099-005-7

Readers of ebooks can buy or view any of these bestsellers by clicking on the live link in the title. Most titles are published in paperback and as an ebook. Paperbacks are available in traditional bookshops. Both print and ebook formats are available online.

Find more titles and sign up to our readers' newsletter at http:// www.johnhuntpublishing.com/christianity. Follow us on Facebook at https://www.facebook.com/ChristianAlternative.